LIBRARY AND INFORMATION SCIENCE EDUCATION IN INDIAN UNIVERSITIES

LIBRARY AND INFORMATION SCIENCE EDUCATION IN INDIAN UNIVERSITIES

B.P. Shrivastava

Commonwealth

Library and Information Science Education in Indian Universities

First Published, 2026

ISBN 81-7169-691-0

Published by
COMMONWEALTH PUBLISHE
4831/24, Govind Lane,
Ansari Road, Darya Ganj,
New Delhi - 110002
Ph. : 23272541, 23242541
e-mail : commonwealthpublishers

Distributed by :
ARJUN PUBLISHING HOUSE
4831/24, Govind Lane,
Ansari Road, Darya Ganj,
New Delhi - 110002
Ph. : 23272541, 23242541
e-mail : arjunbooks2001@gmail.c

Laser Typesetting by :
Dimple Computers
Delhi

Printed at :
Milan Enterprises
Delhi

Dedicated
to
my beloved
MOTHER

PREFACE

There are adequate facilities available in India for the development of man power in Library & Information Science. But the rapid growth of Schools of Library & Information Science has brought in some serious problems also. There is wide variation in resources available to each of these schools and the educational standard maintained by them. The Library schools should provide an efficient organiser, an able administrator and a person who understands the users of the library and their problems.

The book covers the level of education, contents of courses, teaching methods and examination techniques. It also include to research facilities and other academic problems. Such information would be helpful in understanding the needs of the faculty and the library and Information Science education programme can thus be planned and developed in a more realistic and objective manners.

Prof. H.S. Sengar, Director Institute of Distance Education Dr. H.S. Gour University Sagar, motivated me to complete this work. I am thankful to him by heart. Prof. G.D. Bhargava, Prof. H.P. Khare and Dr. M.D. Deoskar helped me to complete this work. I am thankful to them also. In the end I am grateful to Shri B.R. Verma for undertaking the publication

Dr. B.P. Shrivastava

ACKNOWLEDGEMENT

The Library Service in the present time has become sensitive, significant, socially useful and important. It needs well trained, good mannered and experienced personnels. This requires the systematic education in Library science to train personnels for library services. The present study covers the library and information science education in Indian universities with a view to formulate norms in Madhya Pradesh.

I feel immense pleasure in expressing my deep sense of gratitude to my esteemed supervisor Dr. H.S. Sengar University Librarian, Jawaharlal Nehru Library, Dr. Hari Singh Gour Vishwavidyalaya, Sagar and formerly Head of the Department, Library and Information Science for his initial motivation in planning the frame work of the study, constant encouragement and valuable guidance without which it would have not been possible to complete this task. I have received full advantage of his long experience in administration and teaching.

I am highly indebted to Dr. R.G. Prashar, Professor and Head, Department of Library and Information Science and Dean, Faculty of Arts, Dr. Hari Singh Gour Vishwavidyalaya, Sagar for his keen interest, guidance and encouragement.

It is entirely necessary to express my gratitude to Dr. G.D. Bhargava, Retd. Professor and Head, Department of Library and Information Science, Vikram University, Ujjain for his guidance at various stages.

I can not forget to express my gratitude to Shri H.P. Khare, retd. Professor, Education, Dr. Hari Singh Gour Vishwavidyalaya, Sagar for his cooperation, affectionate encouragement and suggestions in the preparation of this study.

I must acknowledge with grateful thanks for the contribution of my colleague Dr. M.D. Deoskar, Lecturer, Education, Dr. Hari Singh Gour Vishwavidyalaya, Sagar who helped me in the preparation of this study. I am much indebted for his kind behaviour, sympathetic attitude and rich experience in research methodology.

I am thankful to Mr. R. K. Gupta, Reader, Department of Library and Information Science, Dr. Hari Singh Gour Vishwavidyalaya, Sagar for his cooperation in the preparation of this work.

I express a deep sense of gratitude to all heads of the departments of library and information science of Indian Universities including those in Madhya Pradesh who cooperated me to complete this study.

The Cooperation of the Library Staff of J.N. Library, Dr. H.S. Gour Vishwavidyalaya, Sagar can not be forgotten and I am thankful to all of them.

My acknowledgements are also due to Mrs. Savita Shrivastava, Lecturer, Govt. Multipurpose Higher Secondary School, Sagar for her cooperation.

I must express my thanks to Mr. Shrikrishna Deousker for typing of the manuscript within a very short period of time.

Mr. M.L. Tiwari, Superintendent, University College of Education, Sagar has been very helpful to me in this research work. I am grateful to him.

Finally, I am thankful to Mr. Pankaj Govil, Sagar Computers, Sagar for helping me in the preparation of graphs.

B.P. Shrivastava

CONTENTS

LIST OF TABLES

LIST OF GRAPHS

1

INTRODUCTION

Introduction

In librarianship, the past history of India, like that of several other countries in the East, is that of a country having libraries with little emphasis on 'library service' in the modern sense. The recognition of the vital role of libraries in the educational, scientific and socio-economic development of the country is, rather a recent phenomenon which came into existence, say, during the past two-three decades.[1]

The need for professionally qualified personnel to manage and run these libraries effectively and efficiently was however duly recognized during the first half of the present century and consequently, library education programmes have been started at several places much before independence in 1947.[2]

In India, more professionally trained librarians are being graduated than elsewhere in the Asian Scene probably due to a longer established tradition of British inspired university organization and scholarship.[3]

There are adequate facilities available in India for the development of manpower in Library Information Science.

---

1. Mangla, P.B., Library and Information Science Education in India. *University News*, 1990, 28, 7.
2. *Ibid.*
3. Gilter, Robert L., Library education—the global scene. George S.Bonn ed. Library education and training in developing countries. Honololu, East-West Centre Press, 1967, p. 9.

But the rapid growth of the schools of Library Information Science has brought in some serious problems also. There is wide variation in the resources available to each of these schools and the educational standards maintained by them. Some of the Library Information schools have been bitterly criticized. The teachers who teach various aspects of library techniques have no field experience. What is more intriguing is that at some universities the entire library science faculty is either holder of Bachelor's Degree or Diploma in Library Science and the department undertakes the teaching of Master's course in Library Science. Under these circumstances the quality of Library Information Science education in India is poor.[4]

In order to meet the challenge of the strong forces that are operating to change the character of library profession, Library Information Science education must be built upon sound intellectual foundation and the librarian needs such training and education which may plant in him the seeds of professional competence. The library schools should produce an efficient organizer, an able administrator, and a person who understands the users of the library and their problems. It is true that at most of the places in India the library schools are trying hard to restructure the training programmes, yet some more efforts have to be made in order to bring about sound arrangement.[5]

History and Development of Library and Information Science abroad: U.K.

Henry Richard Tedder at the 1880 Annual Conference of the Library Association:

'...it is desirable that the Council of the Association

---

4. Srivastava, S.N., Qualitative Improvement in Library Information Science Education. In: R.G. Prasher, ed. University Libraries in India 1980s and beyond. New Delhi, Medallion Press, 1991, pp. 249-50.

5. *Ibid.*

should consider how library assistants may best be aided in their training in the general principles of their profession'.

The above resolution marks the beginning of the formal education for librarians in Britain. It makes two important assumptions: First that it was the responsibility of the newly founded association to supervise the training and education of assistant librarians, and secondly, that librarians has attained the status of a profession. Neither assumption was seriously challenged in the ensuing debate; what was revealed, however, was that training of a sort already existed. At Bolton public library the system was to engage youths for an apprenticeship of two years; at Liverpool the apprenticeship was for five years. The conference, evidently feeling that more than these isolated ventures was needed, adopted Tedder's resolution unanimously and a Committee was appointed to consider the best way in which it could be implemented.[6]

One year later the Committee's recommendations were placed before the London Annual Conference. It proposed a system of examination, consisting of a preliminary examination in the 'ordinary subjects of a sound English Education', followed by a professional examination. In this the Committee was advocating that the Library Association should take the path of the other professional bodies and establish a system of examinations which would raise the professional competence of its members. It was a bold step. The conference, by a small majority, further decided that it was an inappropriate one, and Committee's report was not accepted.[7]

Another committee was appointed and the report was presented again to the conference, this time at Cambridge in 1882. It was preceded by a paper read by Tedder in which he reiterated his belief that librarianship was a profession.

---

6. Bramley, Gerald., A History of Library Education. London : Clive Binglay, 1969, p. 11.
7. *Ibid.*

'....the time has now come when a librarian may without assumption, speak of his occupation as a profession'. He deplored the apprentice schemes which were in existence in several municipal libraries suggesting that they were little better than confidence tricks :

'in plain language a boy is forced to follow a calling he may not like, at wages less than his market value'; and he went on to say that 'we ought to set our faces against any unconscious tendency towards making a trade unions of our profession'. He advocated instead a system of examinations which would distinguish librarianship from a 'handicraft union.[8]

The conference this time adopted in principle the committee's report. It was another three years before it was put into practice and an examination actually held. This followed a timorous announcement in the official journal of the day. The library chronicle, that 'The Library Association of the United Kingdom proposes to hold an examination if candidates present themselves.[9]

Candidates there were, just three in numbers and so in 1885 the first examinations in librarianship were held. The syllabus was as follows: A preliminary examination in: 1. Arithmatic, 2. English, grammar and composition, 3. English history, 4. Geography, 5. English literature.[10]

For a 'Second class certificate': 1. English literature; 2. Someone other European language; 3. Principles of the classification of the Sciences; 4. Elements of bibliography including cataloguing; 5. Library management and administration. In addition, a cataloguing knowledge of atleast two languages besides English was also needed. To obtain the 'first class certificate' the candidate would have to display an advanced knowledge of the five subjects listed in the second class certificate, plus a six subject general literary history. A

---

8. *Ibid.*
9. *Ibid.*
10. *Ibid.*

cataloguing knowledge of three languages and two year's experience completed the requirements.[11]

In the ensuring years several changes were made to the syllabus without attracting members to the examination room in any large numbers. The first change was made in 1890 when a committee was appointed which 'endeavoured to make the examination more popular and less onerous to library assistants'. Two years later, seven candidates braved this new syllabus with 'lamentable result'. In 1894, presumably with the same intention of popularising the examinations, the preliminary test was abolished and the professional section was reduced to three papers only:

1. Bibliography and literary history.
2. Classification, Cataloguing and self-arrangement.
3. Library management.[12]

During the early period London University had the only University School of Librarianship established in 1919. The candidates could prepare for examinations by attending one year's full time course at a school of librarianship. The full time course enables the student to devote his whole energy to study and brings him into close contract with his teachers and fellow students. There are nine colleges offering whole time course. Thus the old apprenticeship system, which had been taken for granted so long, was gradually abandoned and the proportion of part-time students slowly declined after the Second World War.[13]

In the early years of full time library education, the attitude of the profession towards educational matters changed very slowly. Most librarians still thought in terms of the Library Association Charter. They made no reference to education for librarianship as such. In due course of time,

---

11. *Ibid.*
12. *Ibid.*
13. Bhargava, G.D., Librarianship in India and Abroad. New Delhi, Metropolitan, 1977, p. 102.

dialogue between the library schools and the Library Association did help to produce the change of opinion. During the 1969's there has been many fold expansion of full time students and the staff in the library schools.[14]

The development of library education in Great Britain (and Ireland) over the past ten years has been remarkable. In 1960 there was the mondithic structure of the Library Association examination system, which greatly influenced, some would say dictated, the overall teaching in all the library schools, except that at University College, London. By 1964, the picture changed dramatically. Instead of one University school there were four (UCL, Sheffield, Queen's Belfast and Strath clyde); in addition the college of librarianship was being established and this and the school of librarianship, Loughborough Technical College, were to form close working relationships with their neighbouring universities, preparing students for degrees. In addition, a new body, the Council for National Academic Awards was established to validate degrees taught in technical Colleges and polytechnics. The existence of this body led to the establishment of several degrees in library studies and information studies, in addition, to those being offered by the universities. There is now a wide variety of library and information studies degrees and diplomas at the University of Strathclyde, Sheffield, Queen's Belfast, Loughborough, University College, London and University College, Dublin, as well as Polytechnics at Leeds, New-castle, Birmingham, Manchester, Liverpool, polytechnic of North London and the College of Librarianship, Wales.[15]

Research in U.K.

Though research activity in Library and Information Science in the United Kingdom on small scale has been in existence for several decades, yet the major break through has been

14. *Ibid.*
15. Harvard Williams, P., Education for Librarianship in Great Britain, Courses at Loughborough University of Technology In : Venkatappaith, ed. March of Library Science, New Delhi, Vikas Publishing, 1979, pp. 463-64.

made only during the past 15-20 years, more particularly after the establishment of the office of Scientific and Technical Information (OSTI), Department of Education and Science in 1965. OSTI among its major functions and included Research and Development as an important area of activity.[16]

In spite of the fact that the first school of librarianship was established at the University College, London, as early as 1919. No facilities for Ph.D. work were in existence till mid 1960's. The fellowship of the Library Association till 1946 was of course awarded to those who had passed the old final examination but it was possible for a fellow to gain the Honour's Diploma by submission of a satisfactory thesis showing research on some approved subject within the purview of the syllabus. This was no walk over it is found that a number of significant pieces of work were done, some of which were published as books: notably R.C.B. Pastridge's History of the legal adposit of books and Dorothy Norris's History of Cataloguing. Unfortunately, when the new postwar L A syllabus was introduced in 1946 the quality of the research work got diluted simply because the thesis became on 'Essaty' forming part of the final examination.[17]

The establishment of the post-graduate school of Librarianship and Information Science at the University of Sheffield in 1963 can rightly be considered as a turning point in the development of formal research programmes leading to a Ph.D. degree in Library and Information Science in the country. At present there are about 13 library schools extending facilities both for Ph.D. work as well as for carrying out special research projects.[18]

In addition, research projects are being carried out in libraries and information centres by individuals independently

16. Mangla, P.B., Research in Library and Information Science in U.S.A., U.K. and India: an overview. In: Agrawal, S.S. ed. Perspectives in Library and Inf. Science, Vol. 2, Lucknow, Print House, 1982, p. 52.
17. *Ibid.*
18. *Ibid.*

or under the auspicious of professional associations or institutions such as the Library Association, ASLIB, Research and Development Division of the British Library, classification research Group (London), Institute of Information Scientists, etc. The OSTI as such does not exist now because it was transferred to the British Library in 1874 and its various research functions are now carried out by the Research and Development Department of the British Library.[19]

It may be of interest to mention that during the past few years several major information science research projects were as well carried out in laboratories such as the National Physical Laboratory (U.K.) because of the availability of excellent computing facilities. Also, for reasons of staff and of facilities available, several information service research projects have been carried out at two organization dedicated to manipulating large mechanized date bases *viz.* the U.K. Chemical Information Service (CIS) at the University of Nottingham, and the Information Service for Physics, Electrotechnology, Computer and Control (INSPEC) of the Information of Engineers.[20]

Financial support several organizations in the United Kingdom such as government department, and research councils to learned societies, foundations and schools of Library and Information science provide funds for research. Since 1965, OSTI had wide responsibilities for coordination of activities in the field of scientific and technical information with just over $100,000 available during 1965-66 for research grants and contracts, rising to about $8,00,000 in 1973-74. It naturally became the first point of contract for information research workers seeking funds and from its inception provided grants for various research projects, especially in the fields of computational linguistic and information retrieval theory.[21]

---

19. *Ibid.*
20. *Ibid.*
21. *Ibid.*

The great majority of significant research projects in the United Kingdom at present are supported by the British Library Research and Development Department, which covers the whole range of information activities from primary communications through libraries and documentation services to repackaging and referral. Actually this department has been entrusted by the Government with the important responsibility to promote research in Library and Information Science and it functions along broad lines of policy laid down by the British Library Board with regular assistance from an independent Advisory Committee. The vital role this department plays in this context can be best understood by the fact that it has a key position in the government machinery for making national information policy.[22]

Some areas of research during the past 15-20 years can be identified as follows:

1. Development of methodologies for testing the comparative efficiency of the retrieval systems; *e.g.* ASLIB/Granfield Research Project, supported by N.S.F. (USA).
2. Computational linguistics, *e.g.* research work computers effectively for machine translation, automatic indexing, abstracting etc.
3. Communication technology.
4. Information systems and Computer based specialized services.
5. Indexing systems, languages, etc. *e.g.* PRECIS. Thesauri in different areas.
6. Databases; generation, management and services.
7. User's education: User's information requirements.
8. Cost benefit and cost effective studies of operation services, management etc.
9. Information technology and use of computers for

22. *Ibid.*

various purposes in libraries, information systems and services.

10. Micrographics: their production, storage and organization.[23]

Library and Information Science Education in U.S.A.

The professional education of librarians in the United States of America has progressed alongwith fundamentally different lines from the British method of professional training. A key factor in this has been that the American University has all along been prepared to play a full and active part in the education and training of professional man. The European conception of the University as an establishment where the elite are prepared for their ordained place in society, has never been acceptable to the Americans. The university in the U.S.A. may have its origin in Europe, but it has been transformed into something peculiarly American in character. The democratic ideal of the United States is faithfully reflected in her universities. The right of the individual to every opportunity for self improvement is inherent in the U.S. system of higher education, and coupled with this is the convention that individual should be able to develop his education in his own way.[24]

It did, however, raise the American University to the pinnacle of higher education structure. The central government's major contribution to this was the Land Grant Act of 1862, which led to the development of the Land Grant Colleges. These, with the universities, led the way for the development of vocational training for the professions and trades. No attempt was made to separate from each other those vocations which require extensive theoretical instruction' and those which could best be taught by the apprentice method of training. In the egalitarian society, not only were all men equal, but the work which they did was also to be regarded as being of equal importance. As a result, both the professional

23. *Ibid.*, pp. 55-56.
24. Bramley, *op.cit.,* p. 75.

and the vocational schools gradually became attached to the universities. In the case of the newer professions and occupations, however, the association with the university was often of a very tenuous nature—the schools of newer professions occupied a lowly place in the university hierarchy, and exercised little or no influence on university affairs.[25]

In course of time, it was rightly asserted that the role which the library can play in promoting, supporting, extending and enriching formal education is determined very largely by the nature of professionals. In 1876, American Library Association was organized and the American Library Journal became the official organ of the Association. Even after the establishment of this, for several years little attention was given to the matter of training librarians. Melvil Dewey's proposal to train prospective librarians by apprenticeship and a later proposal to establish a school of library economy were not endorsed by the Association. In 1887, Dewey was successful in opening the first school for librarians, the school of Library Economy at Columbia College. In 1889, it became the New York State Library School with Dewey as it's head. The curriculum developed by Dewey was based 'on the routine and typical day-by-day activities of a library and thus was essentially technical and clerical in content.[26]

One the idea of formal library training had taken original shape, other training programmes for librarians were established. In the first two decades of twentieth century, the rapid growth of public and special libraries and of the number of services which they offered and the growing importance of the university library in scholarly research brought added demands for trained librarians.[27]

With the growth in the number and kinds of programmes came the recognition on the part of the established library

25. *Ibid.*, p.76.
26. Bhargava, *op. cit.*, pp. 109.
27. *Ibid.*

schools of the need to establish and maintain standards of instructionery entrance requirements and curriculum. In 1924, the American Library Association established the Board of Education for librarianship to formulate standards and to evaluate and accredit programmes of library education. The Board in 1926, formulated minimum standards for advanced graduate library schools, summer courses, library apprentice and training classes, and the curriculum in school library work.[28]

The structure of library education in United States includes:

1. Undergraduate programme, the majority of which are designed to enable school librarians to meet certification requirements. It offers introductory preparation for library personnel for positions on the level of their preparation and provides a foundation for graduate study in the field of librarianship. It may also provide inservice training opportunities for librarians. It has to develop in students an understanding of the library as a social, cultural and educational agency; a knowledge of the content, evaluation, organization and use of materials and the knowledge of the principles, practices and techniques of library organization and administration.
2. Graduate programme, including master's degree programme, which is the basic professional programme. The programme includes:
   (a) General education which comprises a systematic survey of the various fields of knowledge, concentration in one or more subject fields, and
   (b) Study of professional principles and methods common to the several kinds of librarians and library service.
3. Doctoral programme, which is highly advanced

28. *Ibid.*

professional programme and meant for posts of leaders in library profession.[29]

Research in U.S.A.

U.S.A. was certainly the first country to have started the research programmes in Library and Information Science. As early in 1891 Melvil Dewey, then Director of the New York State Library School at Albany, established the degree of Doctor of Library Science at Columbia a University but it was his intention that the degree should be awarded honoris causa for conspicuous professional achievement rather than for research. There is however no record that the degree was even granted.[30]

It was until the establishment of the Graduate Library School (GLS) at the University of Chicago 1928, with a million dollar grant from the Carneigce Corporation that advanced study and research in Library and Information Science became a reality. The GLS from its very inception included provisions for the award of earned degree of Doctor of Philosophy (Ph.D.) and also ignified heated discussion of what constituted appropriate research in librarianship that would qualify the candidate for the doctor's hood. Until the appointment of Louis R. Wilson as Dean of School in 1932 the programme was however quite unstructured and there were few formal classes. Wilson introduced a substantial measure of formalization initiated the concept of the social sciences as providing the appropriate intellectual foundation for advanced study in librarianship, and insisted that students supplement their study with appropriate courses in other divisions and schools of the university. He gathered around him a remarkable team of specialist teachers and researchers whose writings have a permanent place in library literature: Pierce Butler (Introduction to Library Science, 1933), Douglas Waples (People and Print, 1937 and other Sociological Studies of reading and library use), Casleton B. Jockel (The Government of the

29. *Ibid.*
30. Mangla, *op. cit.*, pp. 47-48.

American Public Library, 1935), William Randall (Principles of College Library Administration, 1936) Leon Cornovsky and James W. Thompson. Also of vital importance was the Library Quarterly in 1936 which was founded and became the major vehicle for publication of important papers on theory and practice of librarianship including accounts on a wide range of research activity.[31]

Because many of the Chicago graduates, especially those during the Wilson era, themselves extend the field of Library education, doctoral programmes later on were heavily influenced by these early development at the GLS. During the 1950's six other library schools, *viz.* Illinois, Michigan, Columbia, Western Reserve, California and Rutgers also started offering the doctoral programmes. Also, there appeared from time to time, doctoral dissertations in the field of librarianship in graduate departments other than library science, *e.g.* Lewis Shere's The American College Library, Sidney Ditzion's Arsenals of a Democratic Culture, Howard McGaw's Marginal punched cards: Their use in college Libraries, to name a few.[32]

During the first thirty years (*i.e.* 1930-1959) of the existence of the research programmes, 129 dissertations were produced of which 80 came from the University of Chicago. Out of these, 45 dealt with the history of books, printing, publishing and the history of individual libraries, whereas other categories were far less frequently represented: library government and administration, 13 studies of technical services, 11 studies of reading and reading interests, 9 studies from the field of content analysis 8 and bibliographic organization, 9. In a number of cases Ph.D. degree was awarded to bibliographical compilation even. These rather scattered and fragmentary statistics clearly show the humanistic origins of library research and the persistence of the humanistic traditions over the years

31. *Ibid.*
32. *Ibid.*

despite the efforts of Wilson and Waplas to channel students into the behavioural sciences.[33]

Recent Developments and Trends

The total number of accredited library schools in the United States today is about 70, and majority of them have provision for doctoral degrees. Though no exact figures of the doctoral theses submitted annually are available, yet on the basis of their listing in the library literature during the past five years or so, it can be concluded that total annual number would be not less than 100. An analysis of the titles of these dissertation indicate that, in addition to being purely historical or descriptive studies, researchers have conducted various other kinds of inquiries including survey and experiment research. They have also adopted operations research techniques in their efforts to quantitatively analyse library problems as a basis for decision making. While these and many other studies in the field have been designed to solve immediate problems and could be classified as applied research. Some studies have been more theoretical in nature. Some of these studies can be identified as basic research because they are directed towards practical applications of knowledge but towards the achievement of fuller understanding of Library and Information science. The distinction between applied and basic research in Library and Information Science has not always been very clear and definite, however.[34]

Factors Contributory to Development of Research in Library and Information Science

As mentioned earlier, though the formal research programme in the United States in Library and Information Science was initiated during the 1930's, yet it was primarily during the 1960's that an extensive break-through was made in this direction. Some of the important contributed factors in this direction are:

33. *Ibid.*
34. *Ibid.*

1. Vast expansion in library collections, number of users, and number of librarians and information scientists;
2. Need to provide specialized services to the users, such as CAS, SDT, etc.;
3. Availability of large financial support from various agencies such as Foundations, NSF, NAST, Library of Congress, NML, and others;
4. Development of research activities in library schools, libraries and information centres;
5. Rapid and innovative developments in information, technology, microreproduction, communical technology, etc.;
6. Active role played by professional associations such as ALA, American Society of Information Scientists, etc.;
7. Vast expansion in research programmes in science and social sciences which made it essential for Library and Information Science to develop new ways and means for information, storage, retrieval and dissemination; and
8. Emergence of research journals for exchange of information.[35]

History and Development of Library and Information Science Education in India

The most important pre-requisite for an efficient library service is proper education for library personnel who are to manage the libraries at every stage. In library education, the past history of India, like that of several other countries of the EAST, is that of a country having libraries but with little emphasis on 'library service in the modern sense'. The recognition of the role of libraries can play in the educational, scientific and socio-economic development of the country is a recent phenomenon. It has taken place during the present

35. *Ibid.*

century more particularly during the past four decades or so.[36] For a long time it was felt that library training was not necessary and some sort of apprentice in a library was sufficient to serve this purpose. The condition in the developed countries had also been the same in the beginning.[37]

The credit for having initiated library training in our country again goes to Baroda. The appointment of W.A. Bordon as a Director of the State Library Department in 1920 led to the starting of library school in 1911. Mr. Bordon had the fortune of being pupil of Dr. Melvil Dewey in his first batch of trained librarians. So he had all the enthusiasm of his master. But this school did not last long.[38] With all this, the beginning of library science training in India dates back to 1910. Carl W. Hintz writes: Formal education in India dates from 1911 and the activities of William Alanson Bordon an American Librarian and the pupil of Melvil Dewey—The Gaekwad of Baroda, Shivaji Rao II, invited Bordon to organise a library system for the state of Baroda. Borden spent three years in Boroda where in addition to developing libraries throughout the state, he started a library school.[39]

The next library classes were also inaugurated by an American librarian and they were also held in an educational institution of university rank. As a Don Dickinson was commissioned by the Government of India in 1916 to organize and catalogue the library of the University of Punjab, and to introduce a course of training in library methods. Dickinson had spent one year at New York state Library School at Albany (1902-3) and he was, like Borden, conversant with the training methods introduced by Dewey. The classes which he set up at the university were on more ambitious lines than those of Borden. The curriculum covered the basic subjects of a professional course: classification, cataloguing, bibliography

36. Bhargava, *op.cit., p.* 118.
37. Kaula, P.N., Library Education in India. In: Kaula, P.N., ed. Library Movement in India, Delhi, Delhi Library Association, 1957, p. 42.
38. *Ibid.*
39. Bhargava, *op.cit.*, pp. 54-55.

and book selection. Dickinson also provided India with its first library text book: The Punjab Library Primes (1916). The University continued to hold classes in librarianship after Dickinson's departure. They consisted of two month's classroom lectures followed by three month's practical library experience in all aspects of library work. The first class held in 1919, attracted twenty-four students and fourteen of those were later awarded a certificate in Modern Library Methods. The course was held again in 1920 and in alternative years thereafter.[40]

In 1929 the Madras Library Association, in conjunction with the University of Madras, began a three month's certificate course in librarianship. The classes were inspired by Dr. S.R. Ranganathan, then the University librarian. The course was taken over by Madras University, which became the first Indian University to offer a comprehensive course in library science when, in 1937, it changed to a one year graduate diploma course.[41] For almost three years the members of the class were mostly school teachers, college lectures and members of the local bodies. In his own words, the objectives of the school was more to establish a modern library outlook than to teach library techniques. But that outlook was to be introduced through the medium of library techniques. It was during these lectures that Ranganathan first enunciated his famous Five Laws of Library Science. The Five Laws appeared in 1931 in the first of his many books on all aspects of library science.[42]

The library profession of India was gradually realizing its responsibilities for the training and education of Indian librarians. Through the medium of the local library associations, a number of courses in librarianship were arranged. The Bengal Library Association arranged a library training camp at

40. Bramely, *op.cit.,* pp. 117-18.
41. *Ibid.*
42. Sharma, O.P., Development of Library Education in India. In: Gujrati, Balwant Singh, ed. Readings in Library Science. Ludhiana, Lyall Book Depot, 1968, p. 42.

Banserbia and in 1937 it established a regular certificate course. The example of the Bengal Library Association was followed by other local library associations: the Bombay Library Association, the Delhi Library Association, the Hyderabad Library Association, the Maharashtra Association and the Gujrat Library Association, all began to offer training classes in Librarianship.[43]

In 1941 the Banaras Hindu University instituted a certificate course and a year later raised it to one year diploma course on the pattern of the Madras School. Bombay University followed Banaras when it started a diploma course in 1946.[44] In the year 1946, Sir Maurice, Gwyer, the then vice Chancellor of the University of Delhi took from S.R. Ranganathan a scheme for establishing a Department of library science at the University of Delhi. The scheme provided for a post-graduate diploma course in Library Science and a Degree course of one year duration after diploma course. Sir Maurice Gwyer also invited Ranganathan, who was then at Banaras Hindu University, to come to Delhi to organize the Department of Library Science. Ranganathan joined the University of Delhi in 1947 and started Diploma course in the same year.[45]

The M.Lib.Sc. (Master of Library Science) Course was, however, started by the University of Delhi in 1948, which incidentally was the first advanced course in Library Science to be started by any university in Commonwealth. Unfortunately, this course was closed down soon after his retirement and was restarted in 1959 by Prof. P.N. Kaula, soon after he was appointed Reader in Library Science, and since then is running upto date. Now the nomenclature of this course at the University of Delhi has been changed from M.Lib.Sc. (Master of Library Science) to the M.L.I.Sc. (Master of Library & Information Science) with slight change in the syllabus.[46]

43. Bramely, *op.cit.,* p. 118.
44. Sharma, *op.cit.,* p. 26.
45. Sharma, Laxmi Prasad, Advanced Training in Library Science in India. In: Venkatappain, ed. March of Library Science; Kaula Festschrift., New Delhi, Vikas, 1979, p. 474.
46. *Ibid.*

Until 1950, besides some institutions offering certificate course, there were only six universities, which offered diploma course in library science. However, the problem of liquidating illiteracy in India, which had been engaging the attention of the responsible authorities, was given very serious attention after the independence, and librarianship came to be recognized as one of the important instruments for the spread of literacy. The Aligarh Muslim University became the first Indian University in the post-independence era to institute a certificate course in 1951, followed by the Maharaja Sayaji Gaekwad University, Baroda, Nagpur University which started diploma course in 1956.[47]

The growth of public libraries of independent India has been remarkably haphazard and casual. The government of India realized this and thus appointed an Advisory Committee for the librarians in 1956 on the recommendation of a 'Seminar on the role of libraries in social education' held in September 1955, organized by the Indian Adult Education Association, at Delhi. The Advisory Committee for libraries has acquired, studied, examined, gathered evidence and after thorough deliberations made certain recommendations in its report governing the structure, the education and training of personal and the administration of the libraries. The Government, however, do not appear to have taken any action on these recommendations so far, but many universities, *viz.* Karnatak, Kerala, Punjab, Rajasthan and Ujjain have already started Diploma or Bachelor programmes in library science.[48]

In 1958, there were only nine universities offering the Diploma course. The fact that, by 1964, the number of such schools has doubled is an indication of the growing interest of intelligencia in library education. The University Grants Commission has now placed librarians on the same salary grades as the teachers in the Colleges and Universities and it now insists that librarians have appropriate degrees. The very

47. Sharma, *op.cit.*, p. 29.
48. *Ibid.*

simple fact that University Grants Commission has recognized the librarians as an important part of the College/University education is an indication that the position has changed lot, which will ultimately affect the training of librarians and will improve standard.[49]

It has made more progress between 1947 and 1980 than during the last one hundred years. Especially after the establishment of the University Grants Commission, several national research organizations, such as CSIR, ICMR, ICAR, BARC, INSDOC, DRTC, ICSSR, ICHR, NISSAT, etc. and expansion of various ministers, a large number of libraries of various types have come into being. In order to train personnel to manage these libraries, library education has also been expanded. By 1980, thirty-five universities had the B.Lib.Sc., twelve upto the level of M.Lib.Sc., and one upto the level of M.Phil. Some had even arrangements for research for the degree of Ph.D.[50]

After the independence, the stimulus for the growth and development of libraries, documentation centres, information centres and of library science education came from the progress in and extension of education, scientific research and programme of socio-economic development in the country. These programmes of national development and reconstruction, started in 1951 with the commencement of the first five year plan, have already progressed through seven such plans. As a result of these developments Library and Information Science (L & IS) today is a well recognised discipline of study and research at the post-graduate level in about 65 universities in the country.[51]

---

49. *Ibid.*
50. Sharma, Jagdish Saran, Librarianship and Library Education in India. Library and Information Science—Current Issues in India; Professor S.N. Shrivastava Festschrift, ed. by Pawan K. Gupta and Usha Kiran, Jaipur; RBSA Publishers, 1986, p. 35.
51. Mangla, P.B., Library and Information Science Education in India—Trends and Issues. University News, Vol. XXVIII, No. 24, 1990, p. 7.

All these 65 universities conduct a one-year post-graduate course leading to the award of Bachelor's degree in library science (B.Lib.Sc.) or Library and Information Science (B.Lib.I.Sc.). About 50 of them have a further one year course for Master's degree in the subject called M.Lib.Sc. or M.L.I.Sc. About 30 universities enrol students for Ph.D. degree and one University, *viz.,* University of Delhi has been conducting a one year post Master's degree course since 1977 leading to the award of M.Phil. degree in the subject.[52]

In addition to universities, the Documentation Research and Training Centre (DRTC), Banglore and Indian Scientific Documentation centres (INSDOC) New Delhi also offer training courses in documentation and/or information science leading to the Associateship of the respective centres.[53]

Presently over 80 universities are running library and information science (LIS) programmes. Important among these universities are Andhra, Madras, Banaras, Bombay, Calcutta, Delhi, M.S. University Baroda, Nagpur, Vikram University Ujjain, Aligarh, Poona, Usmania, Punjab, Rajasthan, Kerala, Karnatak, Lucknow, SNDT University Bombay, Sagar, Burdwan, Gujrat, Jadhavpur, Jiwaji University, Gwalior, Mysore, Shivaji University Kohapur, Gauhati, Varanaseya Sanskrit Vishwavidyalaya Varanasi, Marathawada, Kurukshetra, A.P.S. University, Rewa, Punjabi University Patiala, Ravishanker University, Raipur, Kashmir University, Jabalpur University, Bhagalpur, Banglore, G.N. Deo University Amritsar, Madurai, S.V. University, Tirupati, Udaipur University, Sambalpur University, Calicut University, Gulbarga, Patna, Bundelkhand University Jhansi, Guru Ghasidas University Bilaspur and Jammu University. All of these Universities run B.Lib.I.Sc. course and about one-third of them conduct M.Lib.I.Sc. degree course. Over a dozen of them universities have also instituted doctorate programme. Rajasthan, Punjab, Delhi, Karnatak, Kerala, Banaras, Andhra, Gulbarga, Sagar, Poona, Jiwaji University Gwalior and Nagpur

52. *Ibid.*
53. *Ibid.*

University are running Ph.D. programme in Library and Information Science activity. Besides the Universities, DRTC at Banglore and INSDOC are separately running an advanced course in documentation and information science leading to Associateship in information science. Certificate course in library science are generally run by library associations. Madras, Osmania and Indira Gandhi National Open University run Library Information Science programmes through correspondence. About 2,000 students qualify for B.Lib.I.Sc./ B.Lib.Sc. degree course in India every year and about 200 the Master's degree course. So far about 50 persons have obtained their Ph.D. degree in Library and Information Science and about 20 the M.Phil: degree.[54]

With the alarming increase in number of library schools the quality of the training programmes has certainly got effected adversely. At present there is system of accrediation as such of the library schools at national level. The University Grants Commission is charged with the responsibility of ensuring and maintaining proper academic standards of higher education in the country but till now its role has generally been of a recommendatory nature rather than of an accrediting agency. The need for creating a proper system of accreditation is being felt in the profession quite earnestly but unfortunately a suitable mechanism for this purpose has yet to be devised. Accreditation system for subjects as medicine and law does exist in the country at present.[55]

Certain standards with regard to different aspects such as their qualification, library science library, non-teaching staff, physical facilities etc. have been discussed and useful recommendations made by workshop (1973) and seminar (1977) held at University of Delhi as well as by the University Grants Commission Panel on Library and Information Science.

---

54. Srivastava, S.N., Qualitative improvement in LIS education. In: Prasher, R.G., ed. University libraries in India 1980 and beyond: essays in honour of Prof. T.P. Saxena, New Delhi, Medallion Press, 1991, p. 249.
55. Mangla, *op.cit.,* p. 24.

It has also been emphasized that library schools should conduct courses only at the post-graduate level, and that the undergraduate level courses should be under the purview of, library associations, women's polytechniques or State Libraries.[56]

Research in Library and Information Science in India

Though a developing country, yet India's contribution in Library and Information Science, particularly through the voluminous writings of S.R. Ranganathan are already well recognized all over the world. Library and Information Science is already recognized as a discipline for study and research at the post-graduate level in the universities in the country out of a total of 46 library schools (including the two having courses in Information Science, INSDOC, New Delhi and DRTC, Banglore), about 9 library schools have provision for Ph.D. programme. The library school of the University of Delhi, in addition conducts the M.Phil. programme as well.[57]

Rajasthan, Punjab, Delhi, Karnataka, Kerala, Banaras, Andhra, Gulbarga, Sagar, Poona, Jiwaji University Gwalior and Nagpur University are running Ph.D. programmes in Library and Information Science activity.[58]

Though the first Ph.D. degree in Library and Information Science was awarded by the University of Delhi as early as 1957, yet the development in research work in the country has been rather slow. Because of the vast expansion in libraries and documentation centres in the country during the past 20 years or so, job opportunities greatly improved and the people with good academic and professional qualification were in a position to find good employment without facing much competition. Research qualifications were not prescribed as essential for these job. Certain other factors for lack of research activity in library school include:

1. Small size of the teaching faculty which has to carry a

56. *Ibid.*
57. Mangla, *op.cit.*, p. 56.
58. Srivastava, *op.cit.*, p. 249.

heavy work load of teaching and other academic programmes in the library schools.

2. Lack of research qualifications and experience by teaching faculty and practicing libraries.
3. Lack of financial support in the form of research fellowships, scholarships for young people to work on full time basis.
4. Lack of proper library facilities.
5. Non-availability of research supervisors for topics involving inter-disciplinary research.[59]

Nature of the Research Activity

Unfortunately no comprehensive date is available about the various research projects in Library and Information Science in the country. On the basis of the Input for the International Information System of Research in Documentation (ISORTD) Seetharaman found that during 1968-76, 155 projects were either completed or were in progress in different institutions or organizations. It was found that 92% of the research activity reported emanated from educational institutions such as Universities, DRTC and INSDOC. The remaining 8% were reported from professional associations, information centres and libraries. The research activity in universities, DRTC and INSDOC includes the projects carried out by the students in partial fulfillment for their course requirement. Some of the sponsors for certain projects include U.G.C., ICSSR, National Committee on Science and Technology (NCST) and Tata Energy Research Institute (TERI).[60]

Since India has already built up a fairly vast infrastructure of library and information services and of Library and Information Science education during the past 15-20 years, the need for vigorous research activity need hardly be emphasized. It is hoped that with the financial support and other facilities being provided by universities,

---

59. Mangla, *op.cit.,* p. 56-57.
60. *Ibid.,* pp. 57-58.

and other funding agencies such as DST, ICSSR, CSIR the place of research activity in the country would be much faster in future. Vigorous activity in this connection is not only essential but also urgent because it has been rightly said: 'Research produces knowledge'. Knowledge is needed for understanding and understanding combined with skill leads to effective action.[61]

Need, Significance and Scope of the Study

One of the most significant aspects of the evolution of librarianship in the twentieth century has been the emergence of the library schools as a potent factor in shapping new philosophies and the new attitudes in library profession.

The need for professionally trained personnel was recognised in early decades of the twentieth century. Library training programme were in existence at several places before independence. Much expansion and development in the professional education has, however, taken place after independence in 1947. Consequent to this, library Science Education today, is a well recognized discipline for study of the University level. There are adequate facilities available in universities in India for the development of manpower in Library and Information Science Education. The University Grants Commission has done a lot in this respect. Many Commissions and committees have already given their recommendations for the development of Library and Information Science Education. But the rapid growth of the schools of Library and Information Science has brought some problems also. There is wide variation in the resource available to each of these schools and educational standards maintained by them. There is no uniformity in admission methods, number of seats in each course, staffing pattern, syllabus, teaching methods, workload etc. The intention of the present work is to examine these and some of the implications of this rapid growth in number of schools, noting current trends and possible changes in future. The study shall formulate the norms for Universities of Madhya Pradesh on this basis.

61. *Ibid.*, pp. 59-60.

The study covers the level of education, contents of courses, teaching methods and examination techniques. The study also includes the research facilities, physical facilities and other academic problems. Such information would be helpful in understanding the needs of the faculty and the Library and Information Science Education programme can thus be planned and developed in a more realistic and objective manner.

2

REVIEW OF THE RELATED LITERATURE

The main aim of the present study, as clearly mentioned in the foregoing chapter, is to study the library and information science education in Indian Universities with a view to formulate norms in Madhya Pradesh. Some related studies are briefly revealed as follows:

The popularity of library history as a subject for doctoral investigation was confirmed by Danton (1959) in his study. Danton summaries the problems which Ph.D. students encounter. He cities the benefits to be derived from doctoral study: the contribution which it has made to the knowledge of librarianship, the increased mastery of their subject which librarians have gained the stimulus provided for investigation the actual practice of librarianship.

Dean (1966) studied professional education in Nigeria. The main finding was that by 1965, of the fifty two students who had graduated from the school, twenty six had obtained posts in university libraries compared with the twelve who had sought employment in public library.

Marco (1967) in the result of his survey reports could find little uniformity in entrance requirement, methods of study or in the qualifications which are awarded. A serious threat to the development of doctoral study in librarianship in America has come with the possible reduction in the number of fellowships being awarded by the federal government. Nevertheless librarianship is now firmly established in universities in the U.S.A. as a subject which is worthy of study of doctoral level.

Joseph (1968) found in his investigation that is Britain students were, and still are, experiencing difficulty in securing posts immediately after leaving their library schools. The reasons for this are complex and perhaps the most important single contributory factor was that the examination success rate was much higher now that students were attending full time course.

Harlow (1968) is prepared to concede that selection committees are likely to be impressed by an applicant who has secured a Ph.D. Certainly the indications are that the doctorate is an useful adjunct for those seeking professional advancement. There is a remarkable lack of uniformity in the doctoral programmes now being offered in the United States.

Williams (1969) found in his study that the teaching staff at the institute of librarianship included only one Nigerian lectures, the other three members of the school's faculty being drawn from outside, Nigeria. The library school was not meeting the needs of the public libraries in Nigeria as the bulk of the students sought employment in University libraries.

Bobinski (1969) has given the results of a survey which he made of library school Colloquia in the United States. His investigations reveal a wide variety of approaches in the American library schools in the use of visiting speakers. It concludes that inevitably there will be disadvantages in persuading outside speakers to talk in the library school. Outstanding librarians are not necessarily outstanding speakers. The arrival of visiting speakers as a welcome break from the normal routine, the excessive use of lectures of this kind can disrupt the work of the school.

Kister (1970) studied instructional experiments in educating librarians in intellectual freedom. It is found that these instructional experiments in intellectual freedom is interesting and doubtless valuable at Minnesota, Simmons, UCLA and USC respectively.

Chapman (1970) conducted a survey into British library

school reference teaching. He suggests that there is rather less innovation taking place in the United Kingdom. Twelve British library schools replied his questionnaire. The lecture was apparently extensively used in all the schools: ten out of twelve used the informal lecture (*i.e.* lectures which permitted questions during the lectures), these schools used the formal lecture (questions at the end of the sessions); and seven formal lectures (without questions or discussions). Case studies were however employed by six of schools.

Foskett (1970) suggested that two disciplines are moving closer together is the trend towards using computer assisted methods for teaching classification and cataloguing.

Carroll (1970) considered that foundation of the graduate school was the major contributory factor to the professionalisation of library education.

Lamkin (1971) found that Chief beneficiaries of federal scholarships were white students whose ambitions were often directed towards securing positions in academic libraries.

Grotzinger (1971) found that the two-thirds of American schools of librarianship responding to the enquiry did not, at that time, include field studies in their graduation curriculum. Grotzinger concluded that U.S. library schools were not, in principle, hostile to the concept of field experience, only to its inclusion in the graduation curriculum. The problems of supervising practical work which were considered to be 'prohibitive' and the feeling that practical work was not appropriate in graduate course.

Denis and Hauser (1972) conducted an investigation in to the need for Ph.D. in librarianship in the larger Canadian libraries. Their survey suggested that there could be a demand for between 75 and 100 Ph.Ds in librarianship between the date survey and 1976. The likehood was that the employees covered by the survey would collectively be prepared to send around 85 librarians to doctoral courses. The main difficulty was the lack of financial support which the prospective doctoral student could expect. They concluded that there was a need for Canadian doctoral programmes in librarianship.

White and Mort (1990) surveyed twelve accredited library education programmes in the United States. They studied the reasons for the selection of library schools by the students, types of library expectation upon enrolment, changes from enrolment to graduation and importance of elective course. The findings of this study can be considered to have implications for four groups:' Students, employers/ practitioners, library education programmes and the A.L.A. Committee on Accreditation.

Ahmad (1991) stresses the need for proper training and education of library personnel. It discusses various problems of librarianship in Bangladesh. The main finding of the study is that the profession of librarianship in Bangladesh is at its lowest job, so it fails to attract average people to enroll them in librarianship courses. The necessity of imparting of proper education for librarianship in Bangladesh for providing better librarians to render best possible services is an admitted fact. He suggests that problems are, of course, too many but any organized and planned education and training programmes of librarianship must have permanent value for future prospects in Bangladesh.

Some Indian Studies are as under

Singh (1967) studied the history of library schools in India. His main findings are:

The conditions of library schools in India are not satisfactory, pattern of examination in a almost all the schools is the same. Only in few schools some difference is found in mode of papers and way of examination. There are theory papers in each subject and also practical examination in library classification and cataloguing. Each paper carries 100 marks. Bombay school perhaps is the only school which conducts the practical examination in reference service. Rajasthan school has two term examination carrying 10 percent marks out of the total marks of theory papers. The practical examination in library classification and library cataloguing are performed by question papers in all the schools except Banaras and Rajasthan schools. In these schools the practical examination in both the subjects are performed by the supply of actual books.

Kapoor (1968) made a study of education for librarianship in Indian universities with special reference to pattern of entrants through a survey of 24 universities during the year 1966-67. She used questionnaire as tool. She examined the education for librarianship from the point of view of the students. The major findings are: The student's research interest is quite encouraging, majority of students are interested in research in classification. Thirty five percent (35%) are interested in cataloguing, 35% in reference service, 20% are interested in other subjects. It is, encouraging to see that 'automation' has been given a thought by these future librarians.

Kapoor and Ravinder Kaur (1980) traced the history of library science education in India pre-independence period and post-independence period. It was found in the study, courses in library science of Indian Universities are over crowded with too many subjects as compared to other professional courses, there is no uniformity in library course, departments of the most of the universities do not possess a full time teaching staff and the library science education in our universities is less practice oriented but more theory oriented.

Rao (1981) critically studied the library science education in United States and India. The study covered methods of teaching, course content, role of A.L.A. and U.G.C. Main findings are: The quality of the course content in the United States Library Science Schools is more comprehensive to Indian Library Science Schools, what are all prescribed as basic courses in the United States are the main courses offered in Indian Schools. He suggests, first, the course content should be standardized, and there should be an uniform syllabus in all the library schools throughout the country. The reasons for the high quality of the course content in the United States Library Science schools are: standardization of the course content, uniformity in the syllabus and inclusion of many specialized courses.

Goyal (1981) compared the course content and other aspects of M.Lib.Sc. course at Bombay with those at Delhi University and Banaras Hindu University. He analysed in detail the method of teaching, examination pattern and other related aspects of Bombay University and compared with other universities offering M.Lib.Sc. courses. It was concluded that Master of Library Science Course at Bombay University has started a new experiment where regular classes are not required and no full time teachers are provided.

Kapoor and Banerjee (1985) suggested four years B.Lib.I.Sc. followed by two years M.Lib.I.Sc. and Ph.D. programme.

Gupta (1986) studied educational needs of professional library workers and Library and Information Science education in India. He surveyed a sample of 200 graduates and post-graduates from four library schools of North India. He concludes that problems in the profession need a penetrating look by the library educators in order to tailor their courses and curricula at various levels of library science education. The survey further points out the need to raise the level and standard of library science education on the whole.

Shukla (1987) studied library science teaching for semi-professionals. Out of 93 respondents 52 were graduates whereas 30 and 11 respondents were post-graduates and undergraduates respectively. 34 out of 93 were pursuing certificate course in library science whereas 59 respondents were pursuing Diploma course in library science.

Devarajan (1988) surveyed analysed and provided the recent trends at post-graduate level researches in library science conducted in India in the first half of 1980's.

Kaula (1988) evaluated the education patterns in India, Britain, U.S.A. and Scandinevian countries. He presented an observation on vital issues like professional content of courses, growth of Library Information Science Schools, library facilities and teaching methods.

Tejomurthy (1988) studied the growth of Master of

Library and Information Science dissertation of Vikram University from 1972 to 1987. He presented a subjectwise, and languagewise analyses of the dissertation submitted to the university. He studied 108 dissertations submitted till 1987. It was concluded that bibliographic organization of research work was not properly and adequately undertaken in the country. No systematic effort had been made to disseminate information on dissertations submitted to the universities and institutions.

Mangla (1990) finds that number of full time teachers in library schools in the country is estimated at 250 with 30 professors, 80 readers and 140 lecturers. He finds that these days students with better academic qualifications are admitted in the course, yet it is generally found that number of academically sound students is quite small. Several of these students do not join the course with proper career planning or with a real motivation to work in the profession of Library and Information Science on the priority basis, most of the bright students still prefer to join well accepted professions such as medicine, engineering, banking, accounting etc. Mangla further finds that 90 % of library schools have full time teachers and heads and the other still function under the respective university librarian who has the additional responsibility for the school.

3

PROBLEM, PLAN AND RESEARCH METHOD

Statement of the Problem

Library profession in India at present is passing through a transmission period. It has more progress between 1947 and 1980 than during the last one hundred years. Especially after the establishment of the University Grants Commission, several national research organization such as CSIR, ICMR, ICAR, BARC, INSDOC, DRTC, ICSSR, ICHR, NISSAT etc. and expansion of various ministeries, a large number of libraries of various types have come into being. In order to train personnel to manage these libraries, library education has also been expanded. Presently 80 universities are running library and information programmes at various levels. About four universities are running Library Information Science programme through correspondence.

Many researches have been completed on various aspects of library and information science education but there is no complete research on all aspects of Library Information Science education. There is no uniformity in curriculum, duration of period, admission requirements etc. Except some universities, the majority of universities do not have any uniformity in different aspects.

In Madhya Pradesh seven universities are running Library and Information Science Education on different levels. These universities do not have any uniformity on any aspect. Secondly no study has formulated norms for Library and Information Science education.

Thus, it is proposed to investigate Library and Information Science Education in Indian Universities with a view to formulate norms in Madhya Pradesh.

The problem of the present study is

"A Study of Library and Information Science Education in Indian Universities with a view to formulate Norms in Madhya Pradesh."

Definition of Terms

The terms used in the study needs elaboration and explanation, which is expressed as under:

Library : Oxford dictionary writes about the library, "A place set apart to contain books for reading, study, or reference (Not applied *e.g.* to the shop or warehouse of a book seller)."

Encyclopaedia Britannica mentions about the library, "Library (from Lat Liber, "book") is a collection of written, printed or other graphic material (including films, slides, phonographs, records and taps) organized for use.

Carter V. Good define Library in the following manner

(i) A building or room equipped for housing books and other reading materials of communication for reading, listing or viewing purposes;

(ii) A collection of books of various kinds, and

(iii) A collection of films, recording etc.

Libraries, as S.R. Ranganathan writes, are not mere store houses, they are rich springs from where knowledge flows out to irrigate the wide field of education and culture."

Information Science: Jesse H. Shera and Donald B. Cleveland define the term, 'as the science that investigates the properties and behaviour of information, the forces governing the flow of information and the means of processing information for optimum accessibility and usability. The process includes the origination, dissemination, collection, organization, storage, retrieval, interpretation and use of information. The field is derived from or related to mathematics, logic, linguistic, psychology, Computer technology, Operational research, the graphic arts, communications, library science, management and some other fields.

"Information Science" in the words of H. Borko, is the scientific study of the properties and behaviour of information, the forces governing the flow of information and means of processing it for optimum accessibility and usability".

"Education": Dictionary of Education edited by Carter V. Good defines that:

1. The aggregate of all the processes by means of which a person develops abilities, attitudes, and other forms of behaviour of positive value in the society in which he lives;
2. The social process by which people are subjected to the influence of a selected and controlled environment (especially that of the school so that they may attain social competence and optimum individual development;
3. Ordinarily, a general term for so called, "technical" or more specially classified professional courses offered in higher institutions for the preparation of teachers and relating directly to educational psychology, philosophy and history of education, curriculum, special and general methods, instruction, administration, supervision etc., broadly the total pattern of preparation, formal and informal that the results in the professional growth of teachers;
4. The art of making available to each generation the organized knowledge of the past.

Cyclopedia of Education edited by Paul Monroe writes that, "Speaking generally, education signifies the sum total of processes by mean of which a community or social group, whether small or large, transmits its acquired power and aims which a view to securing its own continuous existence and growth".

University: Webster's New World Dictonary of the American Language defines, "an educational institution of the highest level, variously composed of under-graduates, graduates and professional colleges".

1. An institution of higher education, consisting of a liberal arts college offerings a programme of graduate study, and having usually two or more professional schools or faculties and empowered to confer degrees in various fields of study.
2. An organization that includes the recognised secondary and higher educational institution of a state and certain other institutions of a state and certain other institutions and agencies for education.
3. The institution of higher education that grew up.

Formulate: Odham's Dictionary of English Language defines—"to express in a formula, to express in clear definite terms.

Norms: Odham's Dictionary of English language writes that "the acknowledge standard a model".

Madhya Pradesh: Madhya Pradesh is a state of India.

Objectives of the Study

The present study aims:

1. To access the existing pattern of library and information science education in Indian Universities and M.P.
2. To study the levels of library science education.
3. To study the contents of the courses at the different level in various universities.
4. To examine the strength of the teaching staff and their academic standard.
5. To study work load and teaching methods.
6. To study the procedure of admission, number of seats in each course and also percentage of reservation of seats.

7. To study the examination methods.
8. To study research facilities and library facilities in the department.
9. To formulate Norms for Madhya Pradesh.

Delimitation of the Study

The present investigation is delimited by the following aspects:

1. The study is confined to the Department of Library and Information Science at Indian Universities only.
2. It is delimited to the departments of library and information science opened in Universities upto March 1990 only.
3. It does not cover DRTC and INSDOC for the study.
4. It does not study the certificate course in Library Science and Library Science Teaching through Correspondence.

Plan of the Study

The outline of the plan of the investigation is as under:

The first chapter deals with introduction. It includes history and development of library and information science education in United Kingdom, United States of America and India.

The Second chapter deals with the related studies in United Kingdom, United State of America, India and other countries.

The third chapter deals with problem, plan and research method used.

The fourth chapter deals with analysis and interpretation of data.

Chapter five deals with norms formulated for library and information science education in Madhya Pradesh.

The six chapter deals with conclusions, discussion of results and suggestions.

Research Method

In the present study, the Survey Method has been used. A survey research may be occasioned by a need for some factual information on some aspect of public life or to investigate some cause effect relationship or to make detailed study on some aspects of sociological problems either already studied or afresh.[1] Mr. Wells described 'Survey Research' as a fact finding study dealing chiefly with working class poverty and with the nature and problems of community.

The survey method gathers data from a relatively large number of cases at a particular time. It is not concerned with characteristics of individuals as individuals. It is concerned with the generalized statistics that result when datas are abstracted from a number of individual cases. It is certainly cross sectional.

Six major possibilities of utilization of social science research towards national development can be identified.[2] They are:

1. Social science research throws up valuable background data from which the planner can make his own assessment of the prevailing situation, especially of the magnitude, complexity and ramifications of the problem he has to handle.
2. Carefully designed analytical studies can illuminate critical areas of policy. The overt and covert dimensions of a given problem emerging in such studies provide the planner with a measure of foresight to deal with them effectively and efficiently.
3. These studies open up the possibility of testing the validity of the assumptions that must, of necessity, be

---

1. Srivastava, S.S., Survey research technique. Allahabad, Chaitanya Publishing House, 1971, p. 1.
2. Sharma, B.A.V., Research methods in social sciences. New Delhi, Sterling, 1983, pp. 4-5.

made by the planner in setting his proximate and ultimate objectives.

4. They enable the planner to estimate the possible consequences and cost of the different choices available to them in determining the path for the attainment of their goals.
5. Diagnostic studies suggest where and why particular projects go wrong. Their unintended consequences are also brought to light.
6. Wide dissemination of social science research findings increase general awareness in respect of the situation to be met as well as the policy designed for this purpose. This may enhance the credibility of particular policies and prepare the people for them. It may also help towards building up popular pressures for reformulation of particular policies or for weeding them out altogether.

Some or all these possibilities can be realized provided social research is geared to policy needs and the planner is responsive and sensitive to the research findings.

Research Tool

Factual material or data unknown or untapped so far is essential in every study. They can be obtained from various sources, direct or indirect. It is necessary to adopt or evolve a systematic procedure to collect essential data. Relevant data, adequate in quantity and quality should be collected. They should be sufficient, reliable and valid.

For collecting new unknown data, required for the study of any problem, one may use various devices. For each and every type of research we need certain instruments to gather new facts or to explore new fields. The instruments thus employed as means are called tools. The selection of suitable instruments or tools is of vital importance for successful research.

Different methods used for collection of data in survey

researches may be conveniently grouped into four classes. These are: *(i)* Case study method; *(ii)* observation technique; *(iii)* mail questionnaire, and *(iv)* personal interview.[3]

The investigator has used questionnaire as a tool in the present study.

Questionnaire is widely used for data collection in social research, particularly in surveys. It is a fairly reliable tool for gathering data from large, diverse, varied and scattered social groups. It is used in obtaining objective and qualitative data as well as in gathering information of qualitative nature. It is treated as the 'heart of survey operation'. In specific studies of social environment, the questionnaire is the only research tool used. In most studies it is used in combination with other tools and techniques.[4]

Construction of the Tool

The investigator prepared the questionnaire after interviewing five heads of the departments of library and information science. Even though the investigator interviewed some heads of the departments, it was thought desirable to use questionnaire technique, keeping in view the time factor and financial limitations.

A questionnaire, containing 63 questions, was constructed and then it was given to five heads of the departments for pre-testing.

Necessary modifications were made as per their valuable suggestions. Later on a comprehensive questionnaire was finally prepared for the heads of the departments of library science information science of Indian Universities.

The structure and the contents of the final questionnaire used for the present study can be explained. The questionnaire has 12 major aspects for study. These aspects are:

1. General information, 2. Levels of courses, 3. Contents

3. Srivastava, *op.cit.*, p. 71.
4. Sharma, B.A.V., *op.cit.*, p. 147.

of courses, 4. Examination, 5. Research facilities, 6. Teaching hours and teaching methods, 7. Teaching Staff, 8. Physical facilities, 9. Departmental Library, 10. Fees and Scholarships, 11. Attendance, and 12. Faculty.

Sample and Population

Once the problem has been decided and the questionnaire has been constructed, the next important step which remains with the researcher is to define the population and then specify the sample on which the study is conducted.

"A population is the aggregate of all the cases that confirm to some designated set of specification" (Scllitz Jahoda, Deutsch and Cook, 1963, p. 509).

A sample is a miniature picture of the entire group of aggregate from which it has been taken. A sample in other words, is a small representation of a larger whole. The entire group from which the sample has been taken is known as the "population".[5]

Sampling designs can be broadly classified into two categories:

Probability sampling designs and Non-probability sampling designs.

The probability designs are based on random selection as the fundamental element of control and permit the specification of the precision that can be obtained and the size of the sample required for that purpose. The non-probability designs are based on the judgement of the investigator as the most important element of control.

Hence the investigator here employed probability random sampling technique. The investigator selected 50 Universities out of 65 universities by lottery method.

Administration of the Questionnaire (Tool)

The questionnaire was administered to 50 heads of the

5. Agrawal, Y.P., Sampling methods for social investigation, Ambala, Bharat Vidya Vihar, 1976, p. 10.

departments of library and information science in Indian Universities, out of 50 universities, 39 universities responded.

The size and analysis of the sample is indicated in the following Table 3.1.

Table 3.1
Sample Distribution of Indian Universities

Total Number of Universities conducting Library and Information Science	*Questionnaire administered to Universities*	*Number of Universities responded*	*Percentage*
65	50	39	78%

The Table 3.1 indicates that out of 65 universities conducting library and information science course, the questionnaire was administered to 50 heads of the departments of library and information science in Indian Universities and 78% heads of the departments responded.

In Madhya Pradesh following seven universities are running library and Information Science course at different levels:

1. Dr. Harisingh Gour Vishwavidyalaya, Sagar.
2. Vikram University, Ujjain.
3. Jiwaji University, Gwalior.
4. A.P.S. University, Rewa.
5. Rani Durgawati Vishwavidyalaya, Jabalpur.

Table 3.2
Sample Distribution of Universities in Madhya Pradesh

Total Number of Universities conducting Library and Information Science	*Questionnaire administered to Universities*	*Number of Universities responded*	*Percentage*
7	7	7	100%

6. Ravi Shankar Vishwavidyalaya, Raipur.

7. Guru Ghasi Das University, Bilaspur.

The questionnaire was administered to all of them and cent per cent responded.

The Table 3.2 indicates that questionnaire were administered to seven universities and cent per cent Universities responded in this respect.

4

ANALYSIS OF DATA

Introduction

The questionnaire prepared for the heads of the departments of library and information science in Indian universities were sent to 50 heads of the department of library and information science out of which 39 heads responded.

In Madhya Pradesh, seven universities are running library and information science course at different levels. The questionnaires were sent to all of them. Cent per cent heads of the department responded in this respect.

The data so obtained from Heads of the Department of Library and Information Science of Indian Universities and Universities of Madhya Pradesh were tabulated simultaneously.

The tabulated data of Indian Universities was analysed first and then just after that of Madhya Pradesh was analysed.

Table 4.1
Status of Heads of the Department of Library and Information Science

	No. of Universities		*Percentage*	
Status	*India*	*M.P.*	*India*	*M.P.*
University Professor	14	3	35.89	42.85
University Librarian	10	2	25.64	28.57
Reader	12	1	30.76	14.28
Lecturer	3	1	7.69	14.28
Other	Nil	Nil	Nil	—
Total	39	7	100%	99.98%

The Table 4.1 indicates that 35.89% heads of the department of library and information science of Universities in India are University Professors, while 30.76% and 25.64% heads of the departments are readers and University Librarians respectively. Whereas 7.69% heads are lecturers.

In Madhya Pradesh, 42.85% heads of the department are university professors, but 28.57% heads of the department are university librarians, whereas 14.28% heads are readers and lecturers respectively.

Table 4.2
Age Group of Heads of the Departments

	No. of Heads		*Percentage*	
Age	*India*	*M.P.*	*India*	*M.P.*
Under 30	Nil	Nil	Nil	Nil
31-39	2	1	5.12	14.28
40-49	16	Nil	41.02	Nil
Above 50	21	6	53.84	85.71
Total	39	7	100%	99.99%

Table 4.2 shows that 53.84% heads of the departments in India have attained the age above 50 years and 41.02% heads are in the age group between 40-49 years, whereas 5.12% heads of the department belong to the age group of 31-49 years.

In Madhya Pradesh 85.71% heads of the department have attained the age above 50 years while 14.28% heads are in the age-group between 31-39 years.

Table 4.3
Sexwise Distribution

	No. of Heads		*Percentage*	
Sex	*India*	*M.P.*	*India*	*M.P.*
Male	33	6	84.61	85.71
Female	6	1	15.38	14.28
Total	39	7	100%	99.99%

The Table 4.3 presents the position that 84.61% heads of the department of library and information science of

Universities in India are males whereas 15.38% are females.

In Madhya Pradesh, 85.71% heads are males and 14.28% heads are females in this respect.

Table 4.4
Professional Qualifications of Heads of the Departments

Qualifications	*No. of Heads*		*Percentage*	
	India	*M.P.*	*India*	*M.P.*
B.Lib.I.Sc./Dip. Lib.Sc.	4	1	10.25	14.28
M.Lib.I.Sc.	35	6	89.84	85.71
Total	39	7	100%	99.99%

The Table 4.4 denotes that 89.74% heads of the department in India possess Masters degree in Library and Information Science, whereas 10.25% heads possess B.Lib.I.Sc. degree only.

In Madhya Pradesh, 85.71% and 14.28% heads of the department possess M.Lib.I.Sc. and B.Lb.I.Sc. degree respectively.

Table 4.5
Doctorate Degree Holders

Doctorate	*No. of Heads*		*Percentage*	
	India	*M.P.*	*India*	*M.P.*
Ph.D. (Library Science)	10	1	25.64	14.28
Ph.D. (other subject)	4	2	10.25	28.57
Without Ph.D.	25	4	64.10	57.14
Total	39	7	100%	99.99%

The Table 4.5 reveals that 25.64% heads of the department of library and information science of Universities in India possess Ph.D. degree in Library Science, and 10.25% heads have Ph.D. degree in the subjects other than Library Science, whereas 64.10% heads of the department do not possess doctorate degree in any subject.

In Madhya Pradesh 14.28% heads of the department possess Ph.D. degree in library science and 28.57% heads have Ph.D. degree in the subjects other than library science, while

57.14% heads of the department do not have any doctorate degree in any subject.

Table 4.6
Levels of Courses in Library and Information Science

	No. of Universities		*Percentage*	
Levels	*India*	*M.P.*	*India*	*M.P.*
Ph.D. (Lib.Sc.)	16	3	41.02	42.85
M.Phil.(Lib.Sc.)	1	1	02.56	14.28
M.Lib.I.Sc.	20	5	51.28	71.42
B.Lib.I.Sc.	39	7	100	100
Cert.Lib.Sc.	5	Nil	12.82	Nil
Any other course	Nil	Nil	Nil	Nil

The Table 4.6 shows that facility of Ph.D. in Library and Information Science in India is available in 41.02% University and 02.56% Universities provide M.Phil. (Library Science) facility. Only 51.28% universities are running M.Lib.I.Sc. course. All the Universities run B.Lib.I.Sc. course while 12.82% universities run certificate course in Library and Information science course.

In Madhya Pradesh, 42.85% universities provide facility for Ph.D. in library science and 14.28 universities provide M.Phil. in library science, whereas 71.42% Universities run M.Lib.I.Sc. course. All these universities run B.Lib.I.Sc. course.

Table 4.7
Minimum Qualifications for Admission in Library Science for Ph.D.

	No. of Universities		*Percentage*	
Degree	*India*	*M.P.*	*India*	*M.P.*
M.Lib.I.Sc. only	4	—	25	—
M.Lib.I.Sc.-II	5	3	31.25	100
M.Lib.I.Sc.-55%	6		37.05	—
B.Lib.I.Sc.-II + M.Lib.I.Sc.-II	1		06.25	

The results of this table indicates that minimum qualification for the registration of Ph.D. (Library Science) in 37.5% universities of India is to have 55% marks in M.Lib.Sc.

examination. In 31.25%, 25% and 06.25% universities the minimum qualification is M.Lib.I.Sc second division, M.Lib.I.Sc. only B.Lib.I.Sc. second and M.Lib.I.Sc. second division respectively.

In Madhya Pradesh, in cent per cent universities the minimum qualification for the registration of Ph.D. (Library Science) is to have M.Lib.I.Sc. degree in second division.

Table 4.8
Minimum Qualifications for M.Lib.I.Sc. Admission

	No. of Universities		*Percentage*	
Class	*India*	*M.P.*	*India*	*M.P.*
B.Lib.I.Sc.	8	Nil	40	Nil
B.Lib.I.Sc.-II	7	3	35	60
B.Lib.I.Sc.-50%	5	2	25	40
Total	20	5	100%	100%

The Table 4.8 shows that in 40 universities minimum qualification for admission to M.Lib.I.Sc. course in Inda is B.Lib.I.Sc. In 35% and 25% universities the minimum qualificatins is B.Lib.I.sc. in second division and B.Lib.I.Sc. with 50% marks respectively.

In Madhya Pradesh, the minimum qualification for admission to M.Lib.I.Sc. course in 60% univesities is B.Lib.I.Sc. in second division. In 40% universities is to have B.Lib.I.Sc. degree with 50% marks.

Table 4.9
Minimum Qualification for B.Lib.I.Sc. Admission

	No. of Universities		*Percentage*	
Class	*India*	*M.P.*	*India*	*M.P.*
B.A./B.Sc./B.Com.	1	1	17.94	14.28
B.A./B.Sc./B.Com.-I Divn.	23	4	58.97	57.14
B.A./B.Sc./B.com-50%	9	2	23.07	28.57

The Table 4.9 indicates that minimum qualification for admission to B.Lib.I.Sc. course in 58.97% universities of India is to have bachelor's degree in Arts, Sciènce or Commerce in second division, whereas in 23.07% and 17.94% universities graduates with 50% marks are admitted and also graduates respectively.

In Madhya Pradesh, 57.14% universities admit graduates in Arts, Science or Commerce with second division and 28.57% universities grant admission to graduates with 50% marks and 14.28% universities give admission to graduate only.

Table 4.10
Total Seats for Each Course

	No. of Universities		*Percentage*	
No. of seats	*India*	*M.P.*	*India*	*M.P.*
	Ph. D. (Library and Information Science)			
No limit	4	1	25	33.33
5 per guide	—	—	12.5	—
6 per guide	5	1	31.25	Nil
8 per guide	1	1	06.25	33.33
10 per guide	4		25	
	M. Lib.I.Sc.			
5-7	4		20	
8-10	6	2	30	40
11-13	3	—	15	Nil
14-16	4	1	20	20
17-20	3	2	15	40
	B. Lib.I.Sc.			
10-20	6	1	15.38	14.28
20-30	17	4	43.58	57.14
31-40	7	1	17.94	14.28
41-50	4	Nil	10.25	Nil
51-60	2	Nil	05.12	Nil
61-70	1	1	02.56	14.28
71-80	2	Nil	05.12	Nil

The Table 4.10 denotes the number of seats in Ph.D. (Library Science), M.Lib.I.Sc. and B.Lib.I.Sc. course in Universities of India. In 31.25% University 6 candidates per guide are allowed while in 25% universities total 8 to 10 candidates are allowed whereas in other 25% universities there is no limit of candidates for Ph.D. registration in the

SEATS FOR EACH COURSE

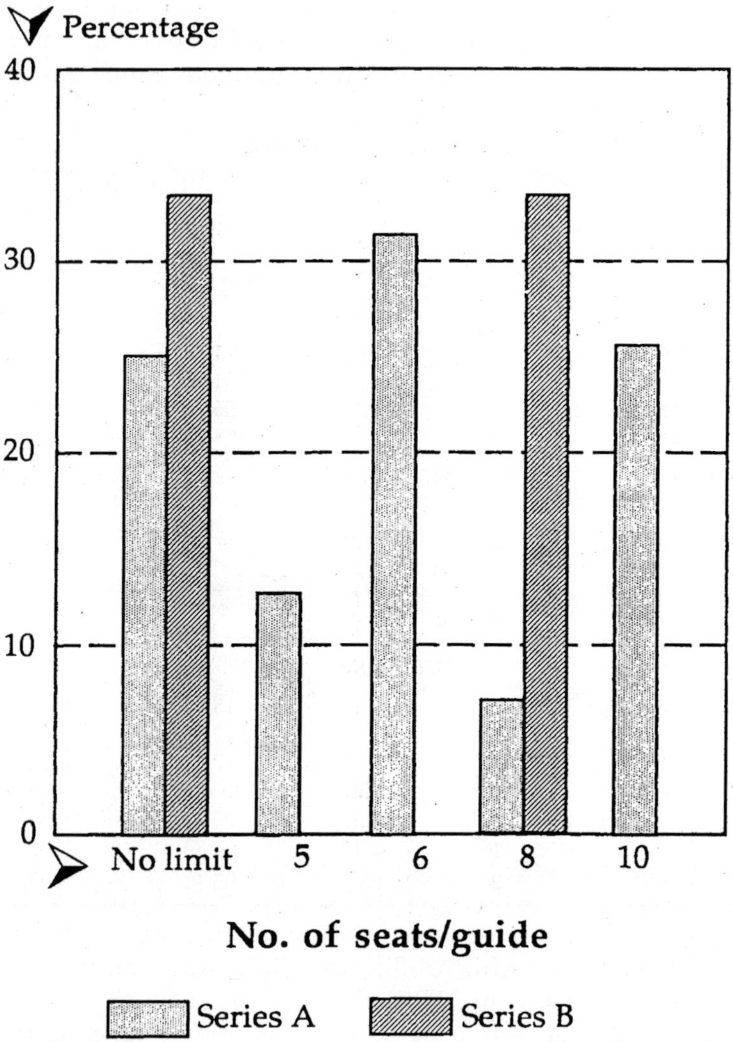

Berlea A - India

Berlea B - M.P.

Ph.D. (Lib. Sc.)

SEATS FOR EACH COURSE

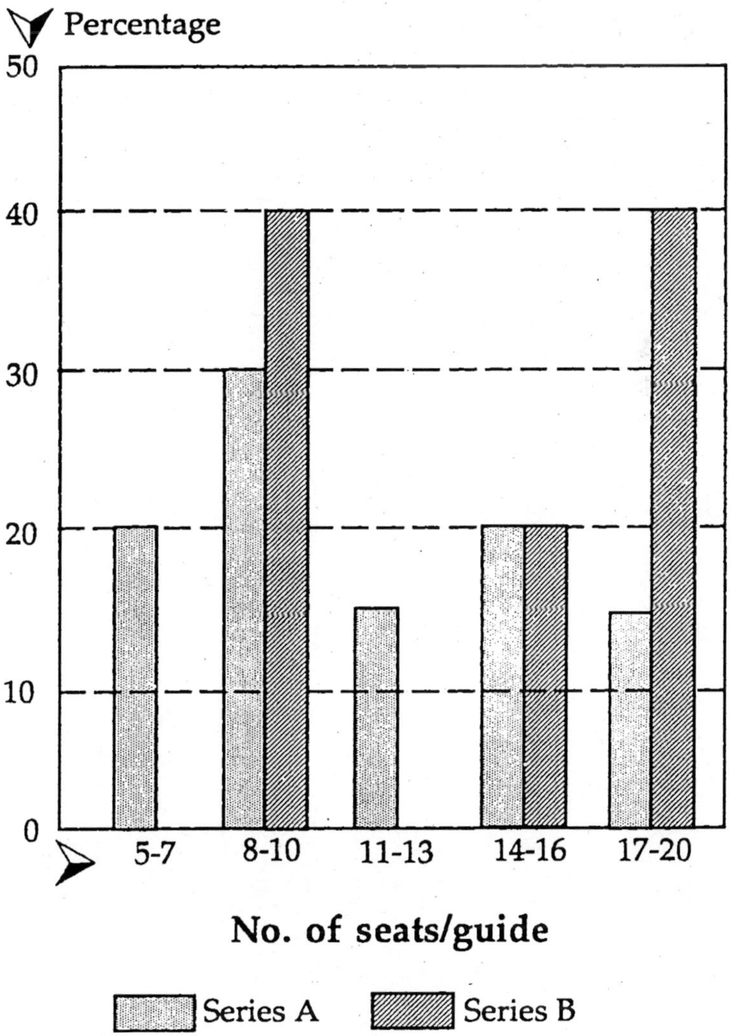

Berlea A - India

Berlea B - M.P.

M.Lib.I.Sc.

SEATS FOR EACH COURSE

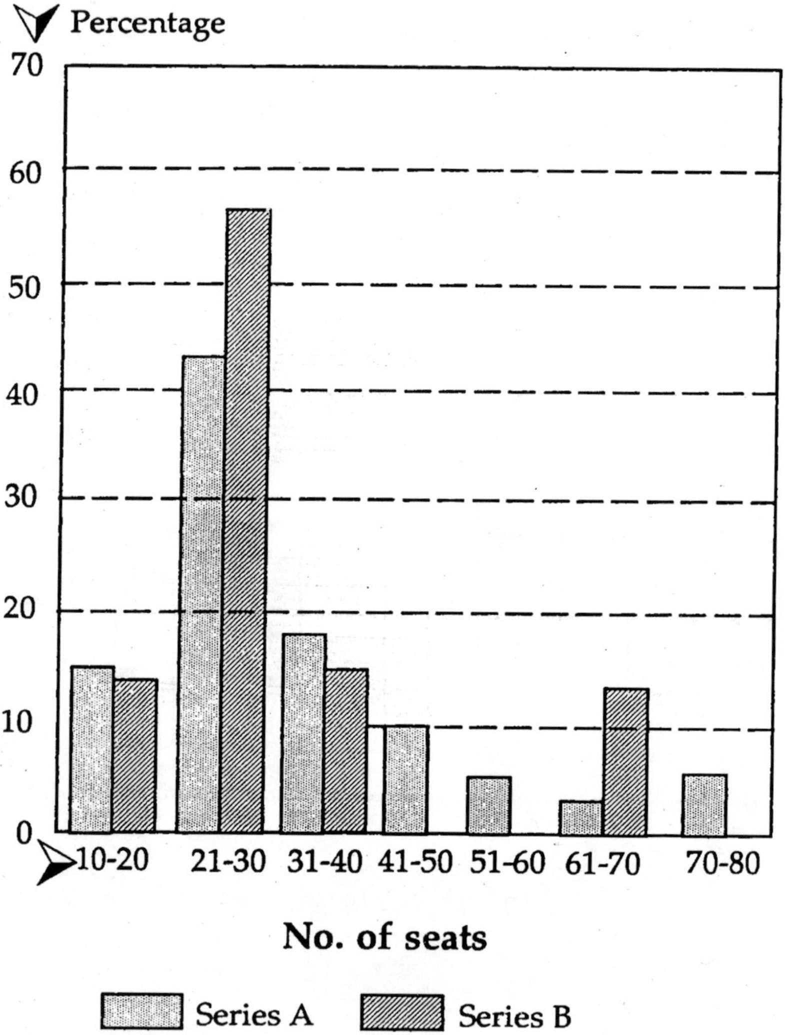

Berlea A - India

Berlea B - M.P.

department of library and information science. It means any number of candidates can be registered for Ph.D. in the department. In 12.5% and 6.25% universities 5 and 8 candidates can be registered per guide respectively.

In Madhya Pradesh, in 33.33% universities 6 per guide and 8 per guide candidates can be registered for Ph.D. respectively. In other 33.33% universities there is no limit of seats for Ph.D. registration in the department. M.Lib.I.Sc.—The total number of seats in 3% universities in India is 8 to 10. In 20% universities it is 5 to 7 and 14 to 16 respectively. In 15% universities the total number of seats is 11 to 13 and 17 to 20 respectively.

In Madhya Pradesh, in 40% universities the number of seats in M.Lib.I.Sc. course is 8 to 10 and in another 40% universities, it is 17 to 20, whereas in 20% universities, the number of seats in 14 to 16.

B.Lib.I.Sc.—In 43.58% universities the number of seats in B.Lib.I.Sc. course is 21 to 30. In 17.94%, 15.38% and 10.25% universities the number of seats are 31 to 40, 10 to 20 and 41 to 50 respectively. In 5.12 universities it is 51 to 60 and 71 to 80 respectively. In 2.56% universities, the number of seats in B.Lib.I.Sc. course is 61 to 70.

In Madhya Pradesh in 57.14% universities the number of seats in B.Lib.I.Sc. course is 21 to 30 whereas in 14.28% universities the number of seats is 10 to 20, 31 to 40 and 61 to 70.

On calculating average number of seats per university have post-graduate course, it is revealed that at National level (India) it comes out to 11.5 and at Madhya Pradesh level it is 14.

This indicates that in M.Lib.I.Sc. course the seats are 12 and at B.Lib.I.Sc. it comes 31 to 40 seats.

The table 4.11 shows that 82.05% universities in India have reservation of seats when 17.94% universities do not have any reservation of seats.

Table 4.11
Reservation of Seats

Reservation	No. of Universities		Percentage	
	India	M.P.	India	M.P.
Yes	32	5	82.05	71.42
No	7	2	17.94	28.57
Total	39	7	100%	99.99%

In Madhya Pradesh, 71.42% universities have reservation of seats while 28.57% universities do not have any reservation as such.

The Table 4.12 indicates the percentage of seats reserved for each category in each course.

M.Lib.I.Sc.—Departmental Candidates

Fourty percent Universities of India have reserved 5% seats for departmental candidates, 30% and 10% universities have 6% to 10% and 31% to 35% seats respectively. Five percent university reserve 16% to 20% and another 5% keep reserved 21% to 5% seats for departmental candidates.

B.Lib.I.Sc.—Departmental Candidates

Fourty percent and 30% universities have reservation of 5% and 6% to 10% seats for departmental candidates respectively. Ten percent universities reserve 51% to 35% seats and another 10% reserve 46% to 50% seats, whereas 5% and 5% universities have 16% to 20% and 21% to 25% seats for departmental candidates respectively.

M.Lib.I.Sc.—SC/ST Candidates

Fourty percent and 30% universities have 11% to 15% and 31% to 35% seats for SC/ST candidates in M.Lib.I.Sc. course. Fifteen and 10% percent universities have 26% to 30% and 36% to 40% seats for SC/ST candidates.

B.Lib.I.Sc. + SC/ST Candidates

Thirty seven and point five percent (37.5%) and 25% universities have 11% to 15% and 16% to 25% seats for SC/ST candidates in B.Lib.I.Sc. course, but in 18.75%, 9.37%, 6.25%

Table 4.12
Categorywise Reservation of Seats and Its Percentage

Number of Universities	Departmental Candidates Upto 5%	6-10%	11-15%	16-20%	21-25%	26-30%	31-35%	36-40%	41-45%	46-50%	Total
					M.Lib.I.Sc.						
India	8 40%	6 30%	Nil	1 05%	1 05%	Nil	2 10%	Nil	Nil	Nil	20
M.P.	Nil	Nil	Nil	2 40%			1 20%				
					B.Lib.I.Sc.						
India	8 40%	6 30%		1 05%	1 05%		2 10%			2 10%	20
M.P.	1 14.28%	1 14.28%		2 28.57%			1 14.28%				5
					M.Lib.I.Sc.—SC/ST						
India	Nil	Nil	8 40%	1 05%		3 15%	6 30%	2 10%	Nil	Nil	20
M.P.				6 60%							
					B.Lib.I.Sc.—SC/ST						
India	Nil	Nil	12 37.5	8 25%	1 3.12%	3 9.37%	6 18.75%	2 6.25%	Nil	Nil	32
M.P.				2 28.57%			3 42.85%				5

and 3.12% universities have 31% to 35%, 26% to 30%, 36% to 40% and 21% to 25% seats for SC/ST candidates in B.Lib.I.Sc. course.

In Madhya Pradesh in M.Lib.I.Sc. for Departmental Candidates

Fourty percent universities have 16% to 20% seats, whereas 20% universities have 31% to 35% seats and in 40% universities there is no seat reserved for departmental candidates.

For departmental candidates in B.Lib.I.Sc. course, 28.57% universities have 16% to 20% seats are reserved while in 14.28%, 14.28% and 14.28% universities have got 5%, 6% to 10% and 31% to 35% seats reserved for departmental candidates respectively. Rest of the universities do not have any seat reserved for departmental candidates.

In M.Lib.I.Sc—SC/ST candidates have got reservation facilities in respect of admission in the following manner:

60% universities in Madhya Pradesh have 16% to 20% seats, while 40% Universities do not have any seat for them in M.Lib.I.Sc. course.

B.Lib.I.Sc. course have given the privilege to SC/ST candidates regarding the reservation facilities as such that, 42.85% and 28.57 universities have 31% to 35% and 16% to 20% seats. Rest of the universities *i.e.* 28.57% do not have any seat for these candidates in this course.

Table 4.13
Procedure of Selection of Candidates for Admission

	No. of Universities		*Percentage*	
Procedure	*India*	*M.P.*	*India*	*M.P.*
On merit	14	1	35.89	14.28
Merit-cum-Interview	10	5	25.64	71.42
Merit-cum-Test	6	1	15.38	14.28
Written Test-cum-Interview	8	—	20.51	—
Written Test only	1	—	22.56	—
Total	39	7	100%	100%

The Table 4.13 reveals that in 35.89% universities of India the candidates are selected on merit to B.Lib.I.Sc. and M.Lib.I.Sc. courses while 25.64% and 20.51% universities select the candidates on merit-cum-interview and written test-cum-interview pattern respectively. On merit-cum-test basis 15.38% universities select them while only 2.56% universities select the candidates through written test.

In Madhya Pradesh, 71.42% universities select candidates on merit-cum-interview pattern whereas 14.28% universities select the candidates on merit basis whereas other 14.28% universities select them on merit-cum-test basis.

Table 4.14
Selection of Departmental Candidates

	No. of Universities		*Percentage*	
Procedure	*India*	*M.P.*	*India*	*M.P.*
Same Procedure	32	7	82.05	100
Not same procedure	7	—	17.94	-
Total	39	7	100%	100%

The Table 4.14 indicates that in 82.05% universities the selection of departmental candidates is the same which is adopted for the direct candidates, but 17.94% universities do not adopt the same procedure.

In Madhya Pradesh, 100% universities adopt the same procedure.

Table 4.15
Procedure of Selection of Departmental Candidates—Other Procedures

	No. of Universities		*Percentage*	
Procedure	*India*	*M.P.*	*India*	*M.P.*
Deputed by libraries	5	—	71.42	—
On merit-among department	1	—	14.28	—
Separate Interview	Nil	—	Nil	—
By seniority among deptt.	1	—	14.28	—
Any other	Nil	—	Nil	—
Total	7	—	100%	—

The Table 4.15 shows that in 71.42% universities, the departmental candidates are deputed by libraries while 14.28% universities select departmental candidates on merit among them. The other 14.28% universities select departmental candidate by seniority among them.

Table 4.16
Duration of Course

No. of Univer-sites	Months									
	Nine		Ten		Twelve		Fourteen		Fifteen	
	No.	%	No.	%	No.	%	No.	%	No.	%
M.Lib.I.Sc.										
India	Nil		9	45	8	40	1	0.5	2	10
M.P.	—	—	3	60	2	40	—	—	—	—
B.Lib.I.Sc.										
India	2	05.12	21	53.84	16	41.02	Nil	—	Nil	—
M.P.	1	14.28	3	42.85	3	42.85	—	—	—	—

The Table 4.16 presents the picture of duration of M.Lib.I.Sc. and B.Lib.I.Sc. courses in India as well as in M.P. Fourty five percent universities in India have duration of period of M.Lib.I.Sc. 10 months, other 40% universities have 12 months' duration whereas in 10% and 5% universities 15 months' and 14 months' duration of period is followed.

The duration of period of B.Lib.I.Sc. in 53.84% Universities is 10 months, but in 41.02% and 5.12% universities it is of 12 and 9 months.

In Madhya Pradesh, the duration of period of M.Lib.I.Sc. course in 60% universities is 10 months and in 40% universities 12 months' duration of period is followed.

The duration of period of B.Lib.I.Sc. course in Madhya Pradesh is 42.85% and 42.85% universities is 10 months and 12 months respectively, but in 14.28% universities it is of 9 months' duration.

The Table 4.17 indicates that 12.82% universities in India run library science course through correspondence while

87.17% universities do not run library science course through correspondence.

Table 4.17
Library Science Course through Correspondence

Course	*No. of Universities*		*Percentage*	
	India	*M.P.*	*India*	*M.P.*
Run correspondence course	5	Nil	12.82	Nil
Do not run correspondence course	34	7	87.17	100

In Madhya Pradesh no university runs library science course through correspondence.

Table 4.18
Levels of Courses Through Correspondence

Levels	*No. of Universities*		*Percentage*	
	India	*M.P.*	*India*	*M.P.*
M.Lib.I.sc.	Nil	Nil	Nil	Nil
B.Lib.I.Sc.	Nil	Nil	Nil	Nil
Cert. Lib. Sc.	5	Nil	100	Nil

The Table 4.18 shows that universities who run correspondence course, run certificate course only in library science through correspondence.

Table 4.19
Contents of Courses—M.Lib.I.Sc.

Theory Papers	*No. of Universities*		*Percentage*	
	India	*M.P.*	*India*	*M.P.*
(1)	*(2)*	*(3)*	*(4)*	*(5)*
1. Universe of knowledge	13	5	65	100
2. Depth Classification/Advance Classification theory	13	5	65	100
3. Advanced Cataloguing theory	13	5	65	100
4. Advanced Reference Service—Part A and B—Bibliography of Literature in SS, Natural Sc., Applied Science or in Humanities	5	3	25	60
5. Documentation and Information Retrieval	4	3	20	60

(Contd...)

(Contd....)

(1)	(2)	(3)	(4)	(5)
6. Documentation and Reference Service	1	—	05	—
7. Documentation	1	—	05	—
8. Fundamentals of Information Science	8	—	40	—
9. Information Centres—Organisation and Management	4	—	20	—
10. Information Storage and Retrieval	5	2	25	40
11. Information systems and programming	2	—	10	—
12. Information Control Techniques	2	—	10	—
13. Information and Communication	3	—	15	—
14. Planning of Information System	1	—	05	—
15. Information Transfer and Dissemination	2	—	10	—
16. Research methods and Information Service	1		05	—
17. Computers and Applications in Libraries	3	1	15	20
18. Research and Statistics	5	—	25	—
19. Organisation of Special Material	1	—	05	—
20. Measurement and Evaluation of Library Services	2	—	10	—
21. Comparative librarianship in Part I and Part II	2	—	10	—
22. Comparative International Librarianship	4	—	20	—
23. Advanced Technical Processing Theory	2	—	10	—
24. System Analysis and Library Management	3	—	15	—
25. System Analysis and Statistics Methods	2	—	10	—
26. Advanced Library System/Library Organisation and Management of either Public Libraries or Academic Libraries or Special Libraries (Any One)	13	—	65	100
27. Advanced Technical Processing Practical	01	—	05	—
28. Classification Practical	13	—	65	—
29. Cataloguing Practical	13	5	65	100
30. Dissertation/Project Report	20	5	100	100
Viva voce	20	5	100	100

Table 4.19 presents the clear picture of contents at M.Lib.I.Sc. course in India. At this level 30 theory and practice papers are taught in different universities which are analysed in the following manner :

1. University of knowledge is taught in 65% universities.
2. In 65% universities the Depth Classification/Advanced Classification Theory is taught.

3. Advanced Cataloguing theory is taught in 65% universities.
4. In 25% universities Advanced reference service Part-A and Part-B Bibliography of literature in Social Science, Natural Science, Applied Science or Humanities is taught.
5. Documentation and Information Retieval is taught in 20% universities.
6. In 5% universities Documentation and reference service is taught.
7. Documentation is taught in 5% universities.
8. In 40% universities Fundamentals of Information Science is taught.
9. Information Centres—Organisation and management is taught in 20% universities.
10. In 25% universities Information Storage retrieval is taught.
11. Information systems and programming is taught in 10% universities.
12. In 10% universities Information control techniques is taught.
13. Information and communication is taught in 15% universities.
14. In 5% Universities Planning of Information Systems is taught.
15. Information Transfer and Dissemination is taught in 10% universities.
16. In 5% universities Research Methods and Information Service is taught.
17. Computers and Its applications in Libraries are taught in 15% universities.
18. In 25% universities Research and Statistics is taught.

19. Organisation of special material is taught in 5% universities.
20. Ten percent universities have facilities of instruction in respect of Measurement and Evaluation of Library Service.
21. Comparative Librarianship in Part I and Part II is taught in 10% universities.
22. In 20% universities International Librarianship is taught.
23. Ten percent universities provide instruction in Advanced Technical processing theory.
24. System analysis and library management is taught in 15% universities.
25. In 10% universities system analysis and statistical method is taught.
26. Advanced Library Organisation and Management/ Library systems of either public Libraries or Academic Libraries or special libraries is taught in 65% universities.
27. In 5% universities Advanced Technical Processing practical is conducted.
28. Advanced Library Classification Practical has been conducted in 65% universities.
29. In 65% universities Advanced Library Cataloguing Practical is organised and done by students.
30. Dissertation and Viva are common in cent per cent universities.

Madhya Pradesh

In Madhya Pradesh, following papers are taught at M.Lib.I.Sc. level in different universities :

1. Universe of knowledge is a common subject which is taught in cent per cent universities of the State.

2. In all the universities of Madhya Pradesh Depth Classification/Advanced Classification theory is taught.
3. Advanced Cataloguing theory is another common subject which is taught in every university of the province.
4. In 60% universities of Madhya Pradesh, Advanced Reference Service Part A and Part B—Bibliography of Literature in Social Science or Natural Science or Applied Science or in Humanities are taught.
5. Documentation and Information retrieval is taught in 60% universities.
6. The forty percent universities have facility to teach Information storage and Information retrieval.
7. In 20% universities Computers and Its Applications are taught.
8. Almost all the universities of Madhya Pradesh have an arrangement to teach Advanced Library Organisation and Management/Library systems of either Public Libraries, academic libraries or special libraries.
9. Advanced Library Classification is taught in cent per cent universities, along with its practice.
10. Cent per cent universities facilitate the teaching in Advanced Library Cataloguing Practice.

Every university cover dissertation/Project Report in its syllabus at M.Lib.I.Sc. level.

The Table 4.20 gives the picture of contents of course taught at B.Lib.I.Sc. level in different universities of India, which is analysed in the following manner:

1. Library classification theory is taught in almost all the universities.
2. Cent per cent Universities have a facility to teach Library Cataloguing theory.

Table 4.20
Contest of Courses: B.Lib.I.Sc.

Theory Papers	No. of Universities		Percentage	
	India	M.P.	India	M.P.
1. Library Classifications Theory	39	7	100	100
2. Library Cataloguing Theory	39	7	100	100
3. Library and Society	27	3	69.23	42.85
4. Library Organisation and Administration	16	1	41.02	14.28
5. Book selection, Bibliography and Reference Service	13	3	33.33	42.85
6. Documentation and Information Science	15	5	38.46	71.42
7. History of Books and Printing	2	—	05.12	—
8. Reference Service	8	—	20.51	—
9. Information work	6	—	15.38	—
10. Bibliography and Literature in a specialized field	3	—	07.69	—
11. Reference and Information service	20	2	51.28	28.57
12. Library Organisation	9	4	23.07	57.14
13. Library Management	21	6	53.84	85.71
14. Physical Bibliography, Reprography and Book Trade	7	—	17.94	—
15. Information Science	5	—	12.82	—
16. Reference Information sources	11	4	28.20	57.14
17. Communication and Society	1	—	02.56	—
18. Comparative librarianship	2	—	05.12	—
19. Foundations of librarianship	2	—	05.12	
20. Library Systems and Management	1	—	02.56	
21. General Knowledge	1	—	02.56	
22. Classification Practical	39	7	100	100
23. Cataloguing practical	39	7	100	100
24. Reference practical	2	—	05.12	
25. Viva	13	1	33.33	14.28

3. In 69.23% universities Library and Society is taught.
4. Library organisation and administration is taught in 41.02% universities.
5. In.33.33% universities book selection, bibliography and reference service is taught.

6. Documentation and information science is taught in 38.46% universities.
7. In 5.12% universities History of books and printing is taught.
8. Reference service is taught in 20.5% universities.
9. In 15.38% universities Information work is taught.
10. Bibliography and literature in a specialized field is taught in 7.69% universities.
11. In 51.28% universities Reference and information service is taught.
12. Library Organisation is taught in 23.07% universities.
13. In 53.84% universities Library Management is taught.
14. Physical bibliography, reprography and book trade is taught in 17.94% universities.
15. In 12.82% universities Information Science is taught.
16. Reference information services is taught in 28.20% universities.
17. Only 02.56% universities provide instruction in Communication and society.
18. Comparative librarianship is taught in 5.12% universities.
19. In 5.12% universities Foundations of librarianship is taught.
20. Library systems and management is taught in 02.56% universities.
21. Only 02.56% universities facilitate the teaching in General knowledge.
22. Every university covers Library classification practical in its under graduate course.
23. Library Cataloguing practical is taught in almost all the universities.

24. Reference practical is a part of syllabus in 5.12% universities.
25. *Viva-voce* has been arranged in 33.33% universities.

Madhya Pradesh

Following papers are taught in different universities of Madhya Pradesh at B.Lib.I.Sc. level:

1. Every university covers Library classification theory in its B.Lib.I.Sc. course and taught in cent per cent universities.
2. Library cataloguing theory is taught in almost all the universities.
3. In 42.85% universities Library and Society is taught.
4. Library organisation and administration is taught in 14.28% universities.
5. In 42.85% universities book selection, bibliography and reference service is taught.
6. Documentation and information science is taught in 71.42% universities.
7. Reference and Information Service is taught in 28.57% universities.
8. Library Organisation has been a part of syllabus at B.Lib.I.Sc. level in 57.14 universities.
9. In 85.71% Universities Library Management/ Administration is taught.
10. Reference and information sources is taught in 57.14% universities.
11. Almost all the universities cover Library classification practical in their B.Lib.I.Sc. syllabus.
12. Library cataloguing practical is taught in every university of the province.
13. Only 14.28% universities have got an arrangement of *viva voce* examination at B.Lib.I.Sc. courses.

Table 4.21

Uniformity of Syllabus in the State

Uniformity	*No. of Universities*		*Percentage*	
	India	*M.P.*	*India*	*M.P.*
Uniformity—B.Lib.I.Sc.	8	—	20.51	
No uniformity	31	7	79.48	100
Uniformity—M.Lib.I.Sc.	3	—	15	—
No uniformity	17	7	85	100

The Table 4.21 reveals that 20.51% universities in India have uniformity in the syllabus at B.Lib.I.Sc. level in the state, while 79.48% universities do not have the uniformity, in this respect.

Uniformity in the syllabus at M.Lib.I.Sc. level is found is 15% universities only, whereas 85% universities do not have any uniformity.

In Madhya Pradesh, no university has uniformity either at B.Lib.I.Sc. or M.Lib.I.Sc. levels.

Table 4.22

Unit System in the Syllabus

System in Syllabus	*No. of Universities*		*Percentage*	
	India	*M.P.*	*India*	*M.P.*
Unit system	10	2	25.64	28.57
No unit system	29	5	74.35	71.42
Total	39	7	100%	100%

The Table 4.22 shows that only 25.64% universities of India have unit system in the syllabus whereas 74.35% universities do not have the unit system in the syllabus.

In Madhya Pradesh, 28.57% Universities have unit system and 71.42% universities do not have unit system in the syllabus.

Table 4.23
Satisfaction with the Contents of Syllabus

Satisfaction	*No. of Universities*		*Percentage*	
	India	*M.P.*	*India*	*M.P.*
	B.Lib.I.Sc.			
Sufficient	11	6	28.20	85.71
Not sufficient	28	1	71.79	14.28
	M.Lib.I.Sc.			
Sufficient	9	5	45	100
Not sufficient	11	—	55	

The Table 4.23 denotes that 28.20% universities of India are satisfied with the contents of syllabus at B.Lib.I.Sc level but 71.29% universities are not satisfied with the contents of syllabus.

At M.Lib.I.Sc. level, 45% universities are satisfied with the contents of syllabus whereas 55% universities are not satisfied.

In Madhya Pradesh, 85.71% universities are satisfied with the contents of syllabus at B.Lib.I.Sc. level and only 14.28% universities are not satisfied.

Almost all the universities are satisfied with the contents of syllabus at M.Lib.I.Sc. level.

Table 4.24
Organising Some Refresher Courses for Practicing Libraries

Need	*No. of Universities*		*Percentage*	
	India	*M.P.*	*India*	*M.P.*
Need	21	6	53.84	85.71
No need	18	1	46.15	14.28
Total	39	7	100	100

The Table 4.24 indicates that 53.84% head of the department of Library Science in Indian universities feel the need to organise some refresher courses for practicing librarians but 46.15% heads do not feel so.

In Madhya Pradesh, 85.71% heads of the department of Library and Information Science feel the need to organise some refresher courses for practicing librarians whereas 14.28% heads do not feel such need.

Table 4.25
Agencies to Organise Refresher Courses

Agencies	No. of Universities		Percentage	
	India	M.P.	India	M.P.
Deptt. of Lib.I.Sc.—Universities	8	4	38.09	66.66
U.G.C.	6	1	28.57	16.66
I.C.S.S.R.	2	—	09.52	—
C.S.I.R.	1	—	04.76	—
I.S.R.O.	0	—	00.00	—
Library Associations	4	1	19.04	16.66
Total	21	6		

The Table 4.25 shows that 66.66% heads of the department suggest department of library and information science to organise refresher courses for the practicing librarians while 28.57%, 19.04%, 9.52% and 4.76% heads of department suggest University Grants Commission, Library Associations, ICSSR and CSIR respectively to organise such courses.

In Madhya Pradesh, 66.66% and 16.66% heads suggest that Department of Library and Information Science and U.G.C. should organise refresher courses whereas other 16.66% heads suggest Library Associations should hold this responsibility.

Table 4.26
Method of Examination

Method of Examination	No. of Universities		Percentage	
	India	M.P.	India	M.P.
	M.Lib.I.Sc.			
Annual Examination	17	4	85	80
Semester Examination	3	1	15	20
Method of Examination—B.Lib.I.Sc.				
Annual Examination	36	7	92.30	100
Semester Examination	3	—	07.69	—

The Table 4.26 indicates that 85% universities take annual examination at M.Lib.I.Sc. level while Semester system to examine the M.Lib.I.Sc. students is followed in 15% universities.

For B.Lib.I.Sc. 92.30% universities follow annual examination method whereas 7.69% universities follow semester system in this respect.

In Madhya Pradesh, 80% and 100% universities follow annual examination system at M.Li.I.Sc. and B.Lib.I.Sc. level respectively. Only 20% universities follow semester system at M.Lib.I.Sc. level.

Table 4.27
Maximum and Minimum Marks Allotted for the Course—M.Lib.I.Sc.

		No. of Universities		*Percentage*	
Marks		*India*	*M.P.*	*India*	*M.P.*
Maximum Marks					
	800	16	3	80	60
	850	1	—	05	
	900	2	2	10	40
	1000	1	—	05	
Minimum for 1st division					
	60%	20	5	100	100
Minimum for IInd division					
	40%	1	—	05	
	45%	1	—	05	
	48%	2	1	10	
	50%	16	5	80	100
Minimum for Pass					
	33%	1	—	05	
	36%	1	—	05	
	40%	3	1	15	20
	50%	15	4	75	80

The Table 4.27 reveals that in 80% Indian universities the maximum marks in M.Lib.I.Sc. examination are 800. In 10% and 5% universities, the maximum marks are 900 and 850 respectively. In other 5% universities, the marks are 1000.

Almost all the universities in India propose 60% marks for first division from the total marks.

In 80% universities, the minimum marks for second division are 50%. In 10% and 5% universities the minimum marks for second division are 48% and 45% respectively. In 5% universities the minimum marks for second division is 40%.

To pass the B.Lib.I.Sc. course 50% minimum marks are proposed or are essential in 75% universities, while in 15% universities, it is 40%, in 5% universities it is 36% and 33% respectively.

In Madhya Pradesh in 60% universities, the maximum marks in M.Lib.I.Sc. examination are 800 but in 40% universities, it is 900 marks.

In all the universities the minimum marks for first division is 60%.

In every university the minimum marks for second division is 50%.

Table 4.28
Maximum and Minimum Marks Allotted for the Course—B.Lib.I.Sc.

		No. of Universities		*Percentage*	
Marks		*India*	*M.P.*	*India*	*M.P.*
Max. Marks					
	800	25	4	64.10	57.14
	850	4	3	10.25	42.85
	900	6		15.38	
	950	2		05.12	
	1000	2		05.12	
Minimum for 1st Division					
	60%	39	7	100	100
Minimum for IInd division					
	40%	2		05.12	
	45%	3		07.69	
	48%	7	1	17.94	14.28
	50%	27	6	69.23	85.71
Minimum for Pass					
	33%	1		02.56	
	36%	1	1	02.56	14.28
	40%	26	6	66.66	85.71
	50%	11		28.20	

In 80% universities of Madhya Pradesh, the minimum marks to pass is 50% whereas in 20% universities, it is 40%.

The Table 4.28 shows that in 64.10% universities of India, the maximum marks in B.Lib.I.Sc. examination are 800. In 15.38% and 10.25% universities, the maximum marks are 900 and 850 respectively. In 5.12% universities the maximum marks are 950 and 100 respectively.

The minimum marks for first division in all universities are 60%.

In 69.23% universities the minimum marks for second division is 50%. In 17.94%, 7.69% and 5.12% universities, are 48%, 45% and 40% respectively.

In 66.66% universities, the minimum marks to pass are 40% while in 28.20%, 2.56% and 2.56% universities, the minimum marks are 50%, 36% and 33% respectively.

In Madhya Pradesh, 800 marks are the maximum marks in 57.14% universities at B.Lib.I.Sc. examination, whereas in 42.85% universities, the maximum marks are 850.

In every university, the minimum marks for first division are 60%.

In 85.71% and 14.28% universities the minimum marks for second division are 50% and 48% respectively.

In 85.71% universities, the minimum marks to pass are 40% while in 14.28% universities, the minimum marks are 36%.

Table 4.29
Moderation of Question Papers

	No. of Universities		*Percentage*	
Moderation	*India*	*M.P.*	*India*	*M.P.*
Moderated	27	4	69.23	57.14
Not moderated	12	3	30.76	42.85

The Table 4.29 shows that in 69.23% universities, the annual question papers are moderated while in 30.76% universities the question papers are not moderated.

In Madhya Pradesh the question papers are moderated, in 57.14% universities and in 42.85% universities the question papers are not moderated.

Table 4.30
Method of Moderation of Question Papers

	No. of Universities		Percentage	
Method	*India*	*M.P.*	*India*	*M.P.*
1. By external and internal	15	2	55.55	50
2. By external only	11	2	40.74	50
3. By internal only	1	—	03.70	—

The Table 4.30 shows that in 55.55% universities the question papers are moderated by both the external and internal examiners. In 40.74% and 3.70% universities, the question papers are moderated by external only and internal only respectively.

In Madhya Pradesh, moderation of question papers are made in 50% universities through external and internal experts both, whereas in 50% universities, the question papers are moderated by external only.

Table 4.31
Research Facility for Ph.D. in Library and Information Science

	No. of Universities		Percentage	
Research Facility	*India*	*M.P.*	*India*	*M.P.*
Research facility available	14	3	35.89	42.85
No research facility	25	4	64.10	57.14

The Table 4.31 indicates that there is no research facility for Ph.D. in library and information science in 64.10% universities of India while 35.89% universities have research facilities.

In Madhya Pradesh, 57.14% universities do not have any research facility, but 42.85% universities have got research facility in Library and Information Science discipline.

The Table 4.32 presents the position of research facilities

in Indian universities through the analysis of the said table. There is no research facility in 72% universities due to not having post graduate department in library and information science whereas 28% universities do not have research facility due to the non-availability of qualified guide.

Table 4.32
Reasons for Absence of Research Facility

Reasons	No. of Universities		Percentage	
	India	M.P.	India	M.P.
No post-graduation in Library and Information Science	18	2	72	50
Not qualified guide	7	2	28	50
No satisfactory library	Nil	—	Nil	—

In Madhya Pradesh, 50% universities have no post-graduation facility and other 50% universities have no qualified guide due to which they can not provide research facility.

Table 4.33
Ph.D. Degree Awarded and Research in Progress

Reasons		No. of Universities		Percentage	
		India	M.P.	India	M.P.
Ph.D. awarded:					
No. of Ph.D. awarded		8	6		85.71
	1-3	4	1	28.57	14.28
	4.-6	2		14.28	
	7-8	Nil			
Ph.D. in progress:					
	1-6	3	2	21.42	28.57
	7-12	2	1	14.28	14.28
	13-18	3		21.42	
	1-.24	Nil		Nil	

The Table 4.33 indicates that one to three Ph.D. degrees in Library and Information Science have been awarded so far in 28.57% universities of India and four to six degrees have been awarded in 14.28% universities.

One to six Ph.D. are in progress in 21.42% universities. Thirteen to eighteen and seven to twelve Ph.Ds are in progress in other 21.42% and 14.28% universities respectively.

PROGRESS IN RESEARCH

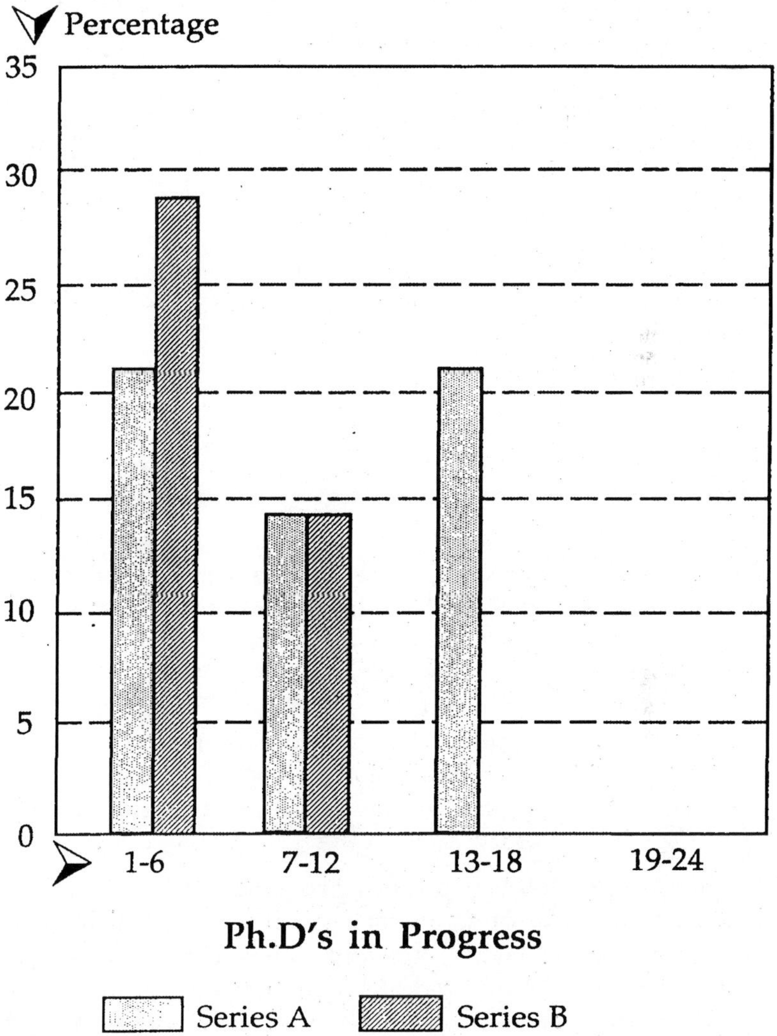

Berlea A - India

Berlea B - M.P.

Ph.D. in progress

In Madhya Pradesh one to three Ph.D. degrees have been awarded in 14.28% universities only. No Ph.D. degree has been awarded in 85.71% universities. One to six Ph.Ds are in progress in 28.57% universities. Seven to twelve Ph.Ds are in progress in 14.28% universities respectively.

Table 4.34
Area of Research Completed and Research in Progress

Areas	*No. of Universities* India	*No. of Universities* M.P.	*Percentage* India	*Percentage* M.P.
Library Classification	4	1	07.27	5
Library Cataloguing	4	1	07.27	5
Library Organisation	7	Nil	12.72	Nil
Library Administration	8	3	14.54	15
Reference Service	Nil	Nil	Nil	Nil
Documentation and Information Science	13	8	23.63	40
Academic Library	12	6	21.81	30
Public Library	7	1	12.72	5
Total	55	20	100%	100%

The Table 4.34 reflects the area of researches completed and research in progress. Out of 55 researches completed and research in progress, 23.63% of them are on documentation and information science, whereas 21.81% and 14.54% researches are on academic library and library administration. On library organization, there are 12.72% researches. The similar percentage is on public library, while 7.27% researches are in the field of library classification and the similar percentage is on library cataloguing.

In Madhya Pradesh, out of 20 researches completed and in progress, 40% of them are on documentation and information science, while 30% and 15% researches are in the field of academic library and library administration while 5% researches are on library classification, library cataloguing and public library respectively.

The Table 4.35 shows that in 66.66% Universities of India, the teaching hours in department of library and information

AREA OF RESEARCHES

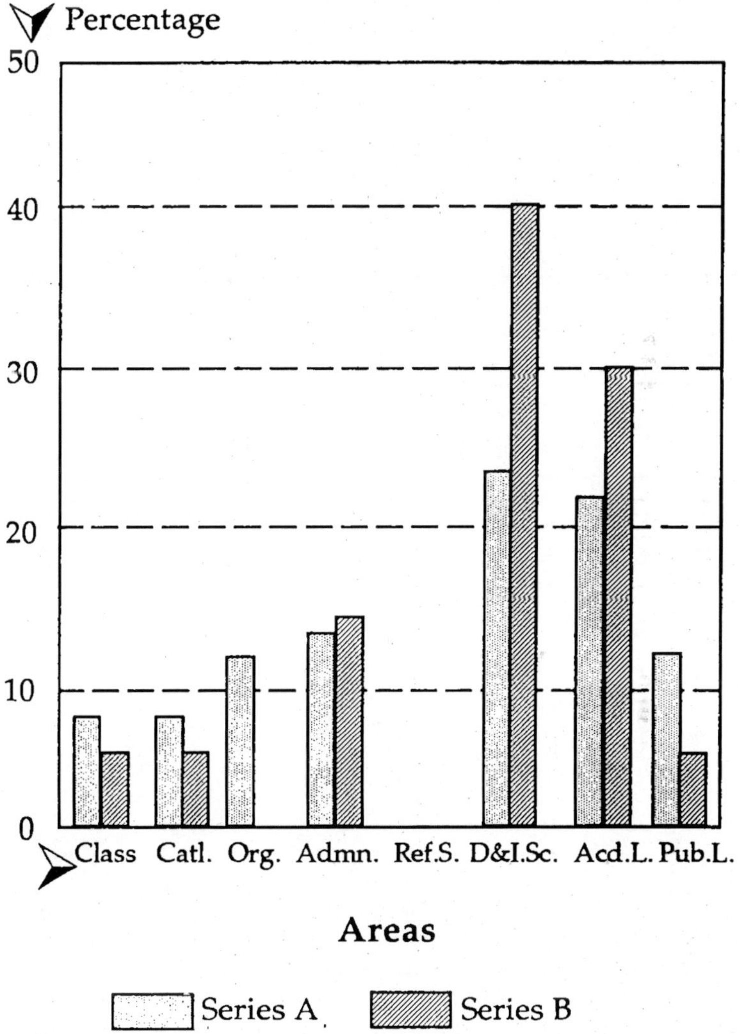

Berlea A - India

Berlea B - M.P.

science are day hours. In 23.07% and 10.25% universities the teaching hours are morning and evening.

In Madhya Pradesh, in 57.14% universities the teaching hours are of morning hours while in 28.57% and 14.28 universities, the teaching hours are day and evening hours respectively.

Table 4.35
Teaching Hours

Hours	No. of Universities		Percentage	
	India	M.P.	India	M.P.
Morning	9	4	23.07	57.14
Day	26	2	66.66	28.57
Evening	4	1	10.25	14.28

Table 4.36
Average Number of Hours Per Week

Number of Hours	No. of Universities		Percentage	
	India	M.P.	India	M.P.
	M.Lib.I.Sc.			
12-18	3	—	15	
19-24	11	4	55	80
25-30	5	1	25	20
31-36	1	—	05	—
	B.Lib.I.Sc.			
12-18	3	—	07.69	—
19-24	24	4	61.53	57.14
25-30	7	—	17.49	—
31-36	3	2	07.69	28.57
37-42	1	—	02.56	—
43-48	1	1	02.56	14.28

The Table 4.36 denotes that average number of hours per week at M.Lib.I.Sc. level are 19 to 24 hours in 55% universities, whereas in 25%, 15% and 5% universities, the number of hours are 25 to 30, 12 to 18 and 31 to 36 hours respectively.

The average number of hours per week at B.Lib.I.Sc. are 19 to 24 hours in 61.53% universities. In 17.94%, 7.69%, 2.56%

AV. NO. OF HRS. PER WEEK

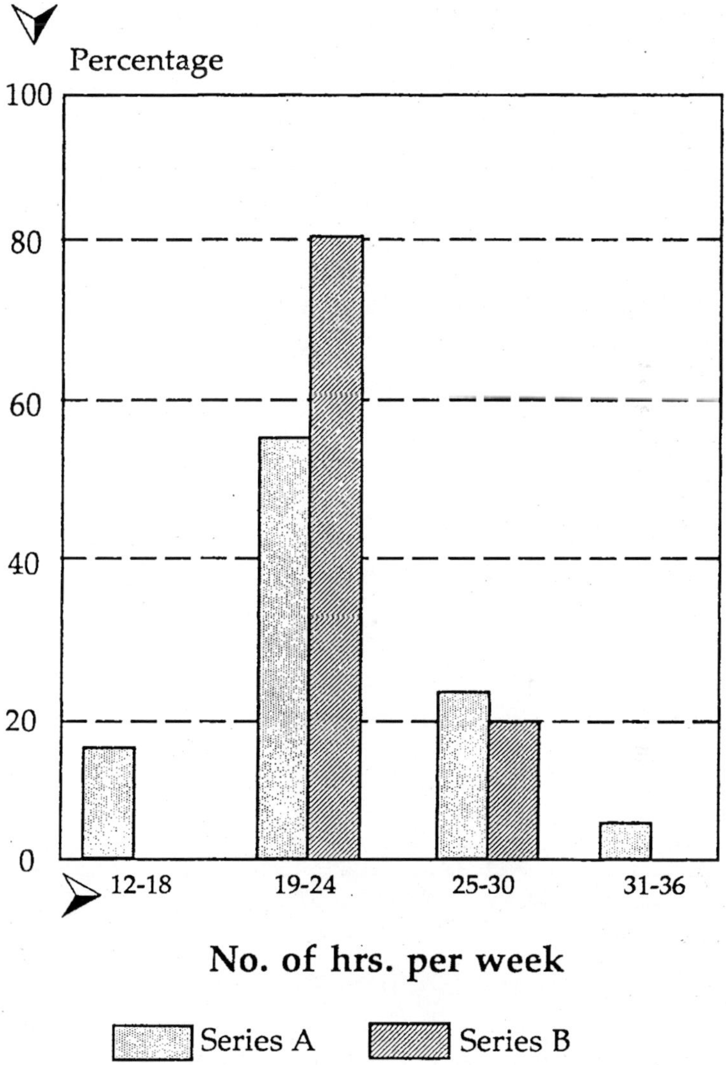

Berlea A - India

Berlea B - M.P.

M.Lib.I.Sc.

AV. NO. OF HOURS PER WEEK

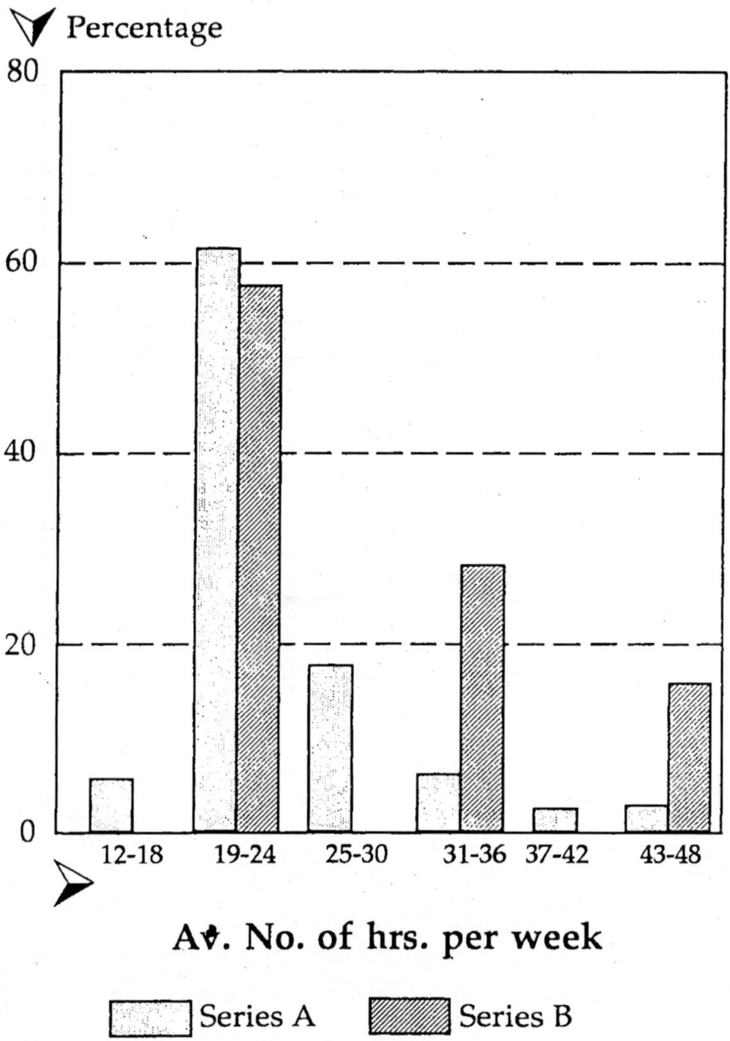

Berlea A - India

Berlea B - M.P.

and 12.56% universities, the average number of hours per week are 25 to 30, 12 to 18, 31 to 36, 37 to 42 and 43 to 48 hours respectively.

In Madhya Pradesh, the average number of hours per week at M.Lib.I.Sc. are 19 to 24 in 80% universities and 25 to 30 hours are in 20% universities.

The average number of hours at B.Lib.I.Sc. level are 19 to 24 hours in 57.14% universities while in 28.57% and 14.28% universities, the average number of hours are 31 to 36 and 43 to 48 hours respectively.

Table 4.37
Methods of Teaching Adopted by the Teachers

Methods	*Order of Preference*							
	India				*M.P.*			
	1	*2*	*3*	*4*	*1*	*2*	*3*	*4*
Lecture	38	1	—	—	6	1	—	—
Seminar	0	25	8	6	0	2	4	1
Tutorial	0	8	24	7	0	0	3	4
Discussion	—	—	—	—	—	—	—	—
Observation	—	—	—	—	—	—	—	—
Apprenticeship	—	—	—	—	—	—	—	—
Practical work	1	11	6	21	1	6	—	—
Any other								

The Table 4.37 indicates that the highest weightage for methods of teaching has ben given to lecture method. The second and third weightage have been given to seminar and tutorial. The practical work is given fourth weightage. No weihtage has been given to discussion, observation and apprenticeship.

The Table 4.38 reveals that in 58.97% universities of India, the medium of instruction is English and in 25.64% universities, the medium is English and Hindi both. In 7.69%, 5.12% and 2.56% universities, the medium of instruction is Gujrati and English both, Hindi, Punjabi and English respectively.

In Madhya Pradesh in 71.42% universities, the medium of instruction is English and Hindi both while in 14.28% and other 14.28% universities the medium of instruction is pure English and purely Hindi respectively.

Table 4.38
Medium of Instruction

	No. of Universities		*Percentage*	
Medium	*India*	*M.P.*	*India*	*M.P.*
English	23	1	58.97	14.28
Hindi	2	1	05.12	14.28
English and Hindi	10	5	25.64	71.42
Punjabi	Nil	Nil	Nil	Nil
Punjabi and English	1	-	02.56	-
Gujrati	Nil	Nil	Nil	Nil
Gujrati and English	3	-	07.69	Nil
Others				

Table 4.39
Difficulty in Teaching in Hindi

	No. of Universities		*Percentage*	
Response	*India*	*M.P.*	*India*	*M.P.*
Difficulty	1		08.33	-
No difficulty	11	6	91.66	100

The Table 4.39 shows that only 8.35% universities feel difficulties in teaching Hindi but 91.66% universities do not feel any difficulty to teach through Hindi.

In Madhya Pradesh no university feel difficulty in teaching through Hindi language

Table 4.40
Difficulties in Medium of Instruction—Hindi

	No. of Universities		*Percentage*	
Difficulties	*India*	*M.P.*	*India*	*M.P.*
Standard books in the subject are not available	1	-	100	-
Technical words in Hindi are difficult	-	-	-	-
Teachers are not well acquainted with the Hindi language	-	-	-	-

The Table 4.40 shows that universities who feel difficulties in teaching through Hindi, almost all of them feel difficulties due to the lack of standard books in the subject. The Universities of Madhya Pradesh have not shown any difficulty regarding the medium of instruction.

The Table 4.41 shows that 71.79% universities arranged the seminars whereas 28.20% universities did not arrange the seminars in Library Science and Information services.

Table 4.41
Seminars Arranged by the Department

	No. of Universities		*Percentage*	
Response	*India*	*M.P.*	*India*	*M.P.*
Deptt. arranged seminars	28	2	71.79	28.57
Department did not arrange seminars	11	5	28.20	71.42

In Madhya Pradesh 28.57% universities arranged the seminars while 71.42% universities did not arrange the seminars.

Table 4.42
Number of Seminars Arranged

	No. of Universities		*Percentage*	
No. of Seminars	*India*	*M.P.*	*India*	*M.P.*
Upto 5	19		67.85	
6 to 10	1	1	03.57	50
11 to 15	4	-	14.28	-
16 to 20	3	1	10.71	50
21 to 25	1	-	03.57	
More than 25	Nil	-	Nil	

The Table 4.42 indicates that 67.85% universities have arranged upto 5 seminars, while 14.28% universities arranged 11 to 15 seminars, 10.71%, 3.57% and 3.57% universities arranged on an average the Universities at India level organised 6 to 7 seminars, per session. The average at Madhya Pradesh level comes to 10 and 16 to 20, 6 to 10 and 21 to 35 seminars respectively.

NO. OF SEMINAR'S ARRANGED

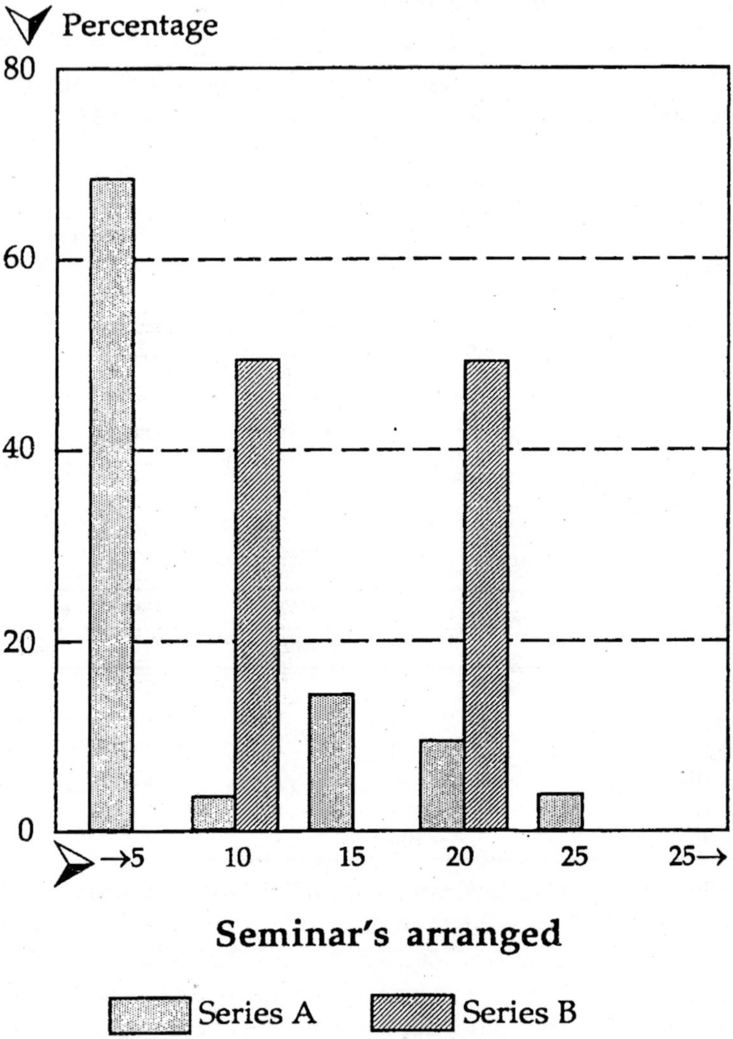

Berlea A - India

Berlea B - M.P.

In Madhya Pradesh, the universities who arranged the seminars are fifty percent and they have arranged 6 to 10 seminars. The other fifty percent universities have arranged 16 to 20 seminars.

On an average, the universities at India level organised 6 to 7 seminars per session. The average at M.P. level comes to 10.

Table 4.43
Full Time Teachers

	No. of Universities		*Percentage*	
Position	*India*	*M.P.*	*India*	*M.P.*
Full time teachers	29	4	74.35	57.14
No full time teachers	10	3	24.64	42.85

The Table 4.43 shows that 74.35% Indian Universities have full time teachers, while 25.64% universities do not have full time teachers.

In Madhya Pradesh 57.14% universities have full time teachers but 42.85% universities do not have full time teachers.

Table 4.44
Strength of Full Time Teachers

			No. of Universities		*Percentage*	
Position			*India*	*M.P.*	*India*	*M.P.*
Professor	1	10	10	3	34.48	75
Reader	1	28	14	2	48.27	50
	2		4	1	13.79	25
	3		2		6.89	
Lecturer	1	65	7	3	24.13	75
	2		13		44.82	
	3		5	1	17.24	25
	4		3		10.34	
	5		1		03.44	
Demonstrator	1		3		10.24	Nil
	2		Nil		Nil	
Total strength		106		10		

NO. OF FULL TIME TEACHERS

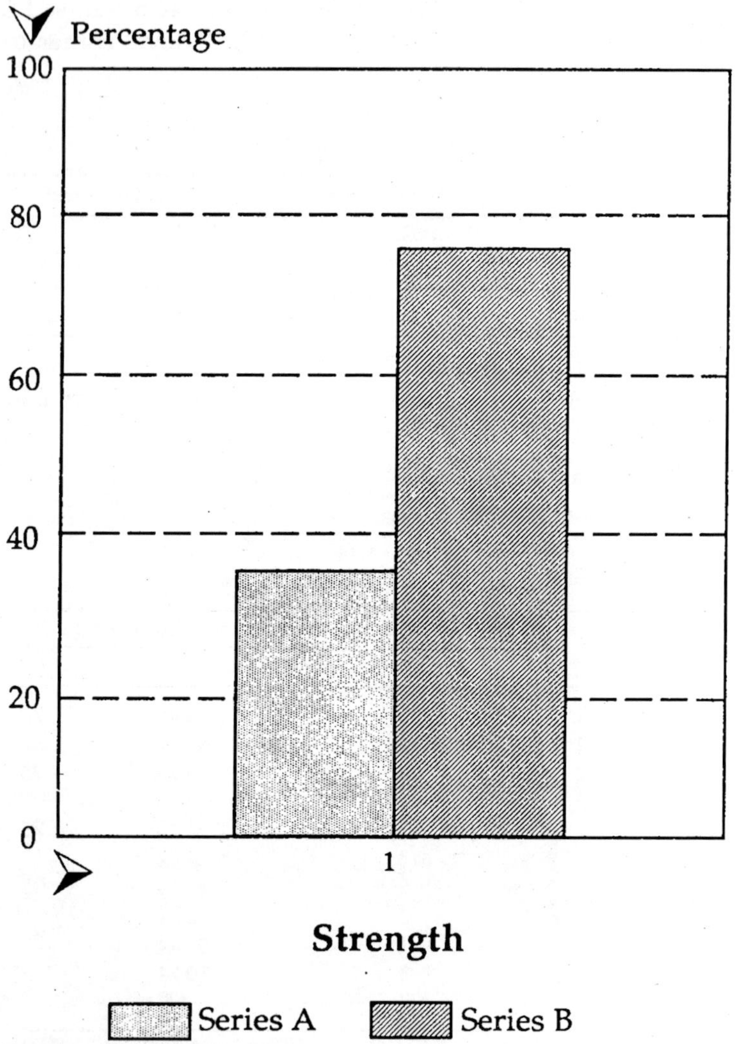

Berlea A - India

Berlea B - M.P.

PROFESSORS

NO. OF FULL TIME TEACHERS

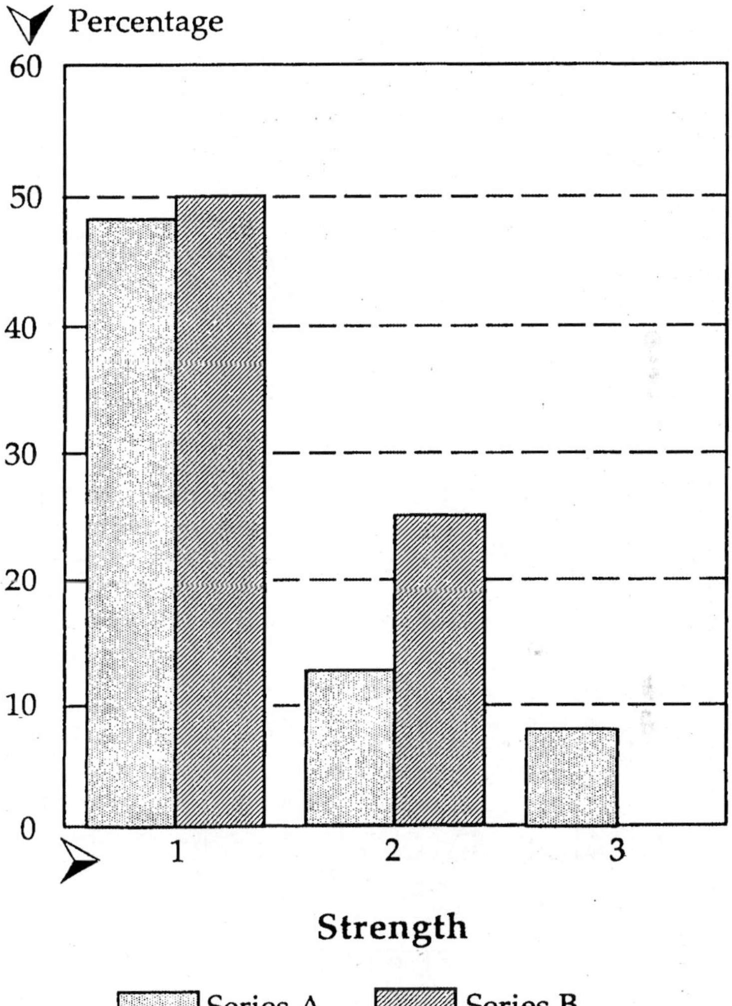

Berlea A - India

Berlea B - M.P.

READERS

NO. OF FULL TIME TEACHERS

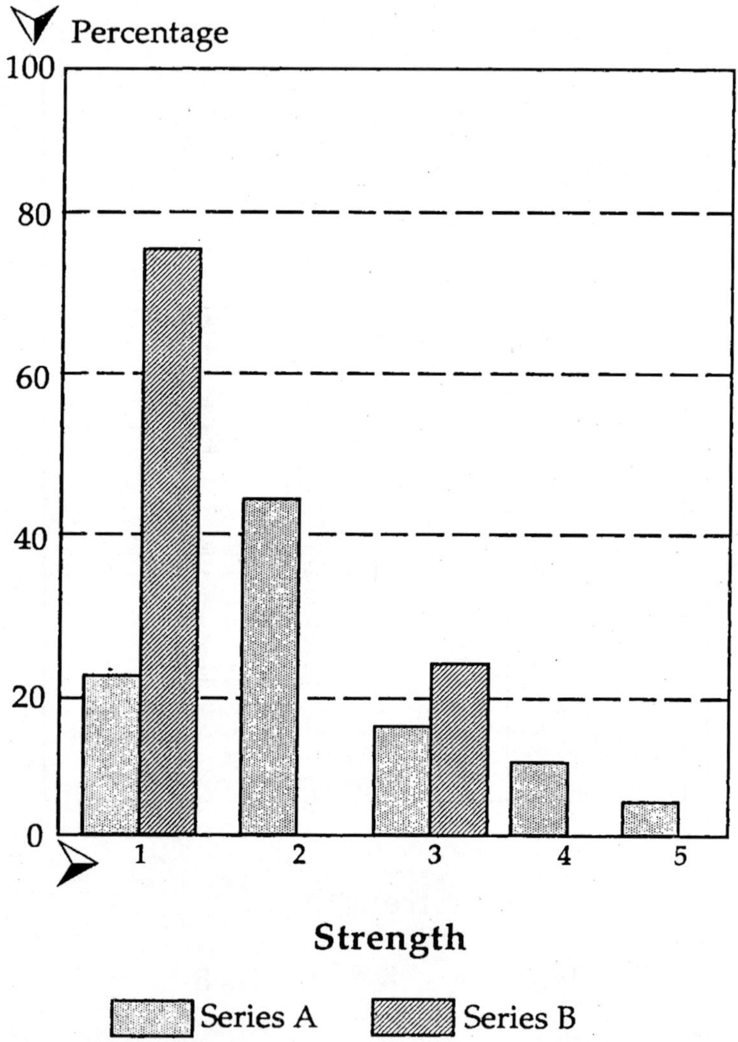

Berlea A - India

Berlea B - M.P.

LECTURERS

NO. OF FULL TIME TEACHERS

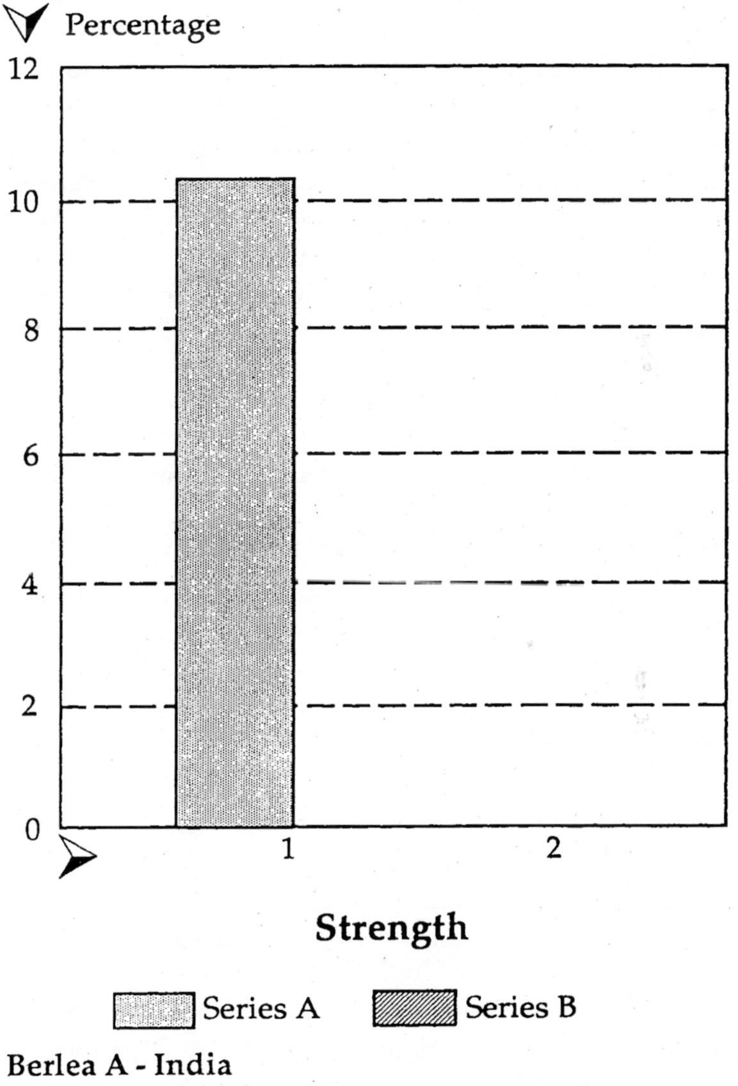

Berlea A - India

Berlea B - M.P.

DEMONSTRATORS

The Table 4.44 reveals that there are total 106 full time teachers in library and information science departments in 29 universities (Table 4.43). There is one University Professor in 34.48% universities and there is no professor in rest of the universities.

There is one reader in 48.27% universities, two to three readers are in 13.79% and 6.89% universities respectively.

There are two lectures in 44.87% universities, one lecturer in 24.13% universities. There are three, four and five lecturers in 17.24%, 10.34% and 3.44% universities respectively. There is one demonstratorin 10.34% universities.

In Madhya Pradesh the position in this respect as such, there is one university professor in 75% universities, one reader is in 50% universities, two readers in 25% universities respectively.

There is one lecturer in 75% universities, three lecturers in 25% universities. There is no demonstrator in any university.

Table 4.45
Academic Qualifications of the Teachers

	No. of Universities		*Percentage*	
Qualifications	*India*	*M.P.*	*India*	*M.P.*
B.A.,. B.Sc., B.Com.	12		11.32	
M.A., M.Sc., M.Com.	94	12	88.67	100
B.Lib.I.Sc./Diploma in Lib.Sc.	106	12	100	100
M.Lib.I.Sc.	71	12	66.98	100
Ph.D. (Lib.Sc.)	21	2	19.81	16.66
Ph.D. (Other subject	2	1	01.88	08.33
M.Phil. (Lib.Sc.)	1		00.94	-

The Table 4.45 indicates that 11.32% teachers in library and information science of India are graduates *i.e.* B.A., B.Sc., B.Com., 88.67% teachers possess M.A., M.Sc., M.Com. degrees.

Almost all the teachers possess B.Lib.I.Sc./Diploma in library science. M.Lib.I.Sc. Qualifications are possessed by 66.98% teachers which mean 33.01% teachers are not post-graduates in library and information science.

ACADEMIC QUALIFICATIONS

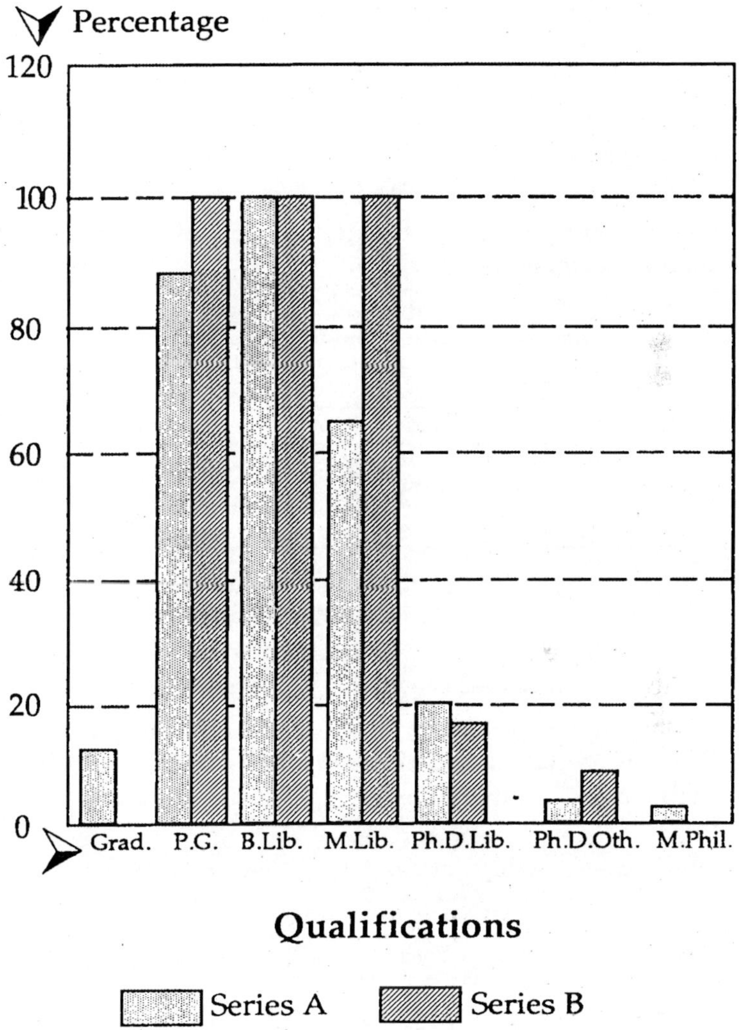

Berlea A - India

Berlea B - M.P.

TEACHERS

Only 19.81% teachers possess Ph.D. degree in library science, 1.88% teachers possess Ph.D. degree in the subject other than library science and 0.94% teachers possess M.Phil. degree in library science.

In Madhya Pradesh, every teacher possess M.A., M.Sc., M.Com. degrees and also they possess M.Lib.I.Sc. degree.

Only 16.66% teachers in M.P. possess Ph.D. degree in library science, whereas 8.33% teachers possess Ph.D. degree in the subject other than library science.

No teacher possess M.Phil. Degree in library and information science.

Table 4.46
Number of Teachers Guiding Research

No. of Teachers	*No. of Universities*		*Percentage*	
	India	*M.P.*	*India*	*M.P.*
One	7	2	17.94	28.57
Two	4	2	10.25	28.57
Three	3		07.69	

The Table 4.46 denotes that there is one teacher guiding research work at Ph.D. level in 17.94% universities and there are two and three teachers guiding research in 10.25% and 7.69% universities respectively.

In Madhya Pradesh, there is one teacher guiding research in 28.57% universities and there are two teachers guiding research in 28.57% universities.

Table 4.46(a)
Research Fellowship in Library and Information Science

Fellowship	*No. of Universities*		*Percentage*	
	India	*M.P.*	*India*	*M.P.*
Fellowship provided	4	1	10.25	14.28
Fellowship not provided	35	6	89.74	85.71

The Table 4.46(a) shows that research fellowships were provided in 10.25% universities whereas no fellowship was provided in 89.74% universities.

In Madhya Pradesh, research fellowships were provided in 14.28% universities but no fellowship was provided in 85.71 universities.

The Table 4.47 shows the position regarding the full time teachers in the universities. In 50% universities 3 to 4 teachers 40% and 1% universities have 1 to 2 and 5 to 6 part time teachers.

In Madhya Pradesh, all the Universities (100%) have 3 to 4 part time teachers.

Table 4.47
Number of Part Time Teachers

	No. of Universities		*Percentage*	
Number	*India*	*M.P.*	*India*	*M.P.*
1 - 2	4	-	40	-
3 - 4	5	3	50	100
5 - 6	1	-	01	
7 - 8	Nil	-	Nil	-
9 - 10	Nil	-	Nil	-

Table 4.48
Payment of Honorarium to Part-Time Teachers

	No. of Universities		*Percentage*	
Payment	*India*	*M.P.*	*India*	*M.P.*
Honorarium paid	10	3	100	100
Honorarium not paid	Nil	-	Nil	-

The Table 4.48 indicates that every university in India as well as in Madhya Pradesh pay honorarium to part-time teachers.

The Table 4.49 shows that 20% universities of India pay upto Rs. 250 per month to part time teachers.

The other 20% universities pay Rs. 251 to Rs. 500 per month. The 10% universities pay Rs. 501 to Rs. 750, Rs. 751 to Rs, 1,000 and Rs. 1,000 to Rs. 1,250 per month respectively. The 10% universities pay Rs. 15, Rs. 25 and Rs. 40 per lecture to part time teachers respectively.

Table 4.49
Amount of Honorarium Paid to Part Time Teachers

	No. of Universities		*Percentage*	
Amount	*India*	*M.P.*	*India*	*M.P.*
Per month upto Rs. 250	2	1	20	33.33
Rs. 251- to 500	2	2	20	66.66
Rs. 501 to 750	1	-	10	-
Rs. 751 to 1000	1	-	10	-
Rs. 1000 to 1250	1	-	10	-
Percentage of basic pay	Nil			
Per lecture Rs. 15	1	-	10	-
Rs. 25	1	-	10	-
Rs. 40	1	-	10	

In Madhya Pradesh, Rs. 251 to Rs. 500 per month are paid to part time teachers in 66.66% universities, and in 33.33 universities Rs. 250 per month are paid.

Table 4.50
Workload of Teachers

	No. of Universities		*Percentage*	
Workload	*India*	*M.P.*	*India*	*M.P.*
Professor Upto 6 periods per week	2	-	20	-
7-12 per week	6	2	60	66.66
13-18 per week	2	1	20	33.33
19-24 per week	-	-	-	-
Reader Upto 6 periods per week	1	-	0.05	-
7-12 per week	12	-	60	-
13-18 per week	5	2	25%	66.66
19-24 per week	2	1	10	33.33
Lecturer Upto 6 per week	1	-	02.56	
7-12 per week	7	-	17.94	
13-18 per week	17	1	43.58	25
19-24 per week	4	3	10.25	75
Part time teachers upto 6 per week	4	-	40	-
7-12 per week	4	2	40	66.66
13-18 per week	2	1	20	33.33
19-24 per week	Nil	-	Nil	-
Demonstrator upto 6 per week	Nil	-	Nil	
7-12 per week	3	-	100	-

WORKLOAD OF TEACHERS

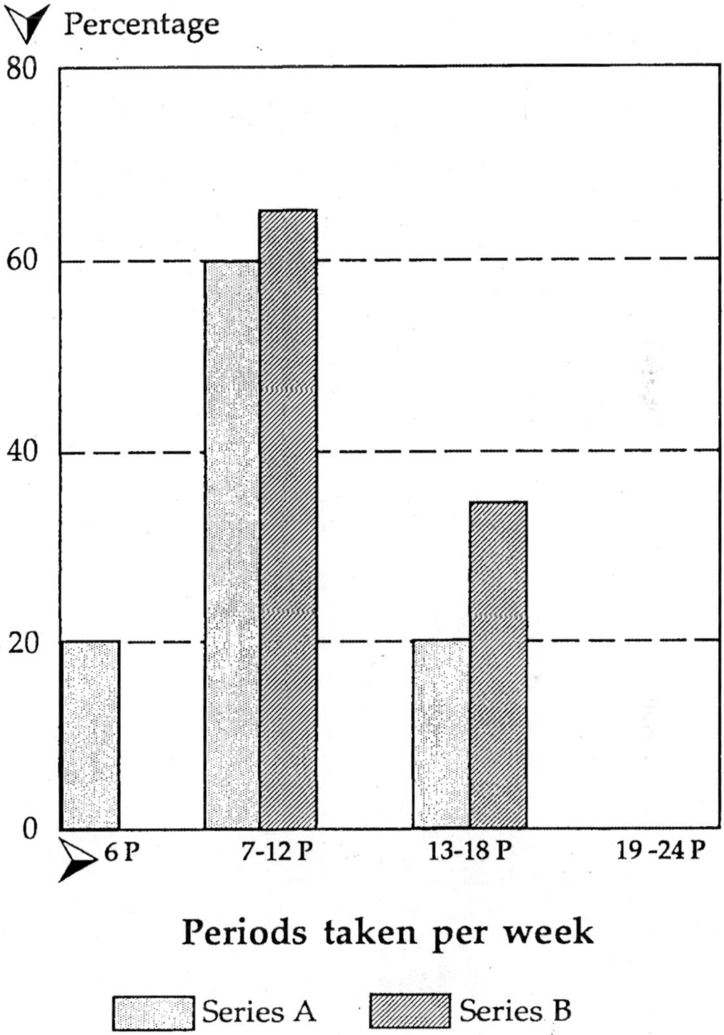

Berlea A - India

Berlea B - M.P.

WORKLOAD OF TEACHERS

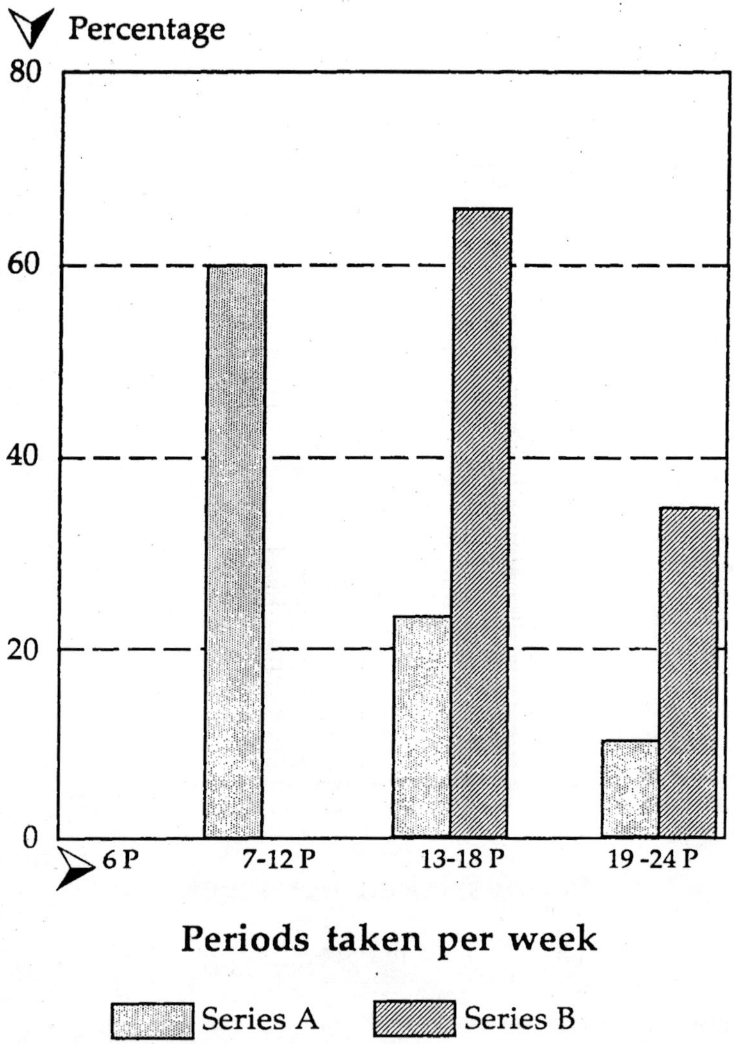

Berlea A - India

Berlea B - M.P.

READERS

WORKLOAD OF TEACHERS

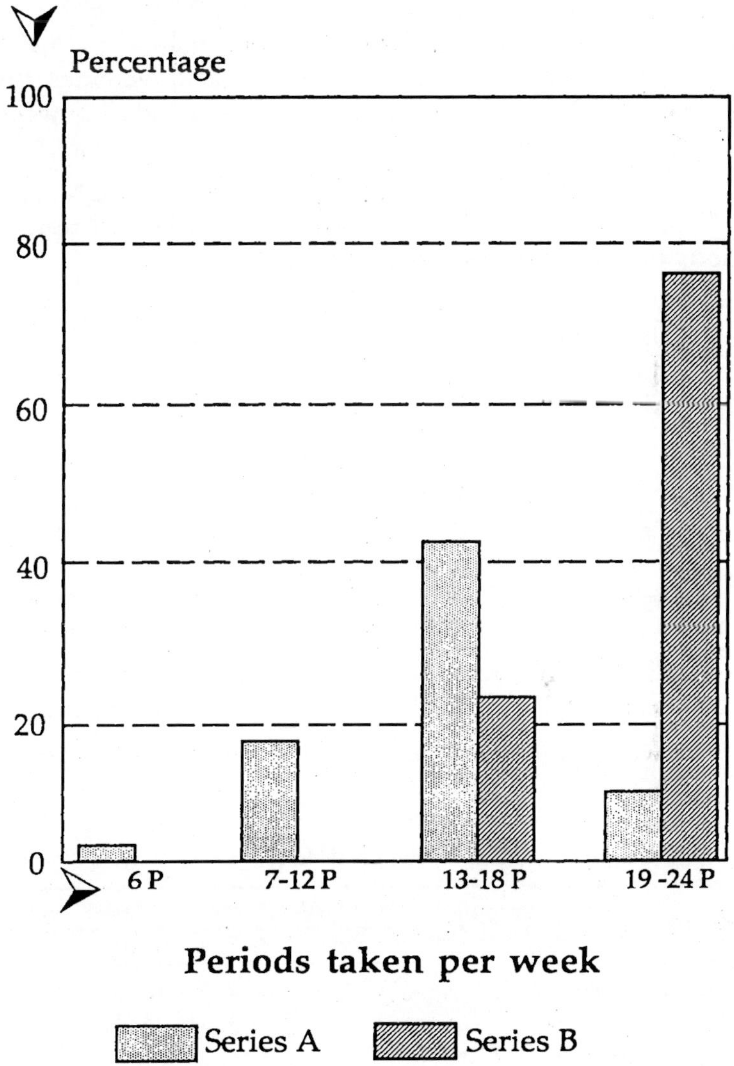

Berlea A - India

Berlea B - M.P.

LECTURERS

The Table 4.50 depicts that the teaching workload of Professors in 60% universities is 7 to 12 periods per week. In 20% universities it is 13 to 18 and upto 6p periods per week.

The workload of readers in 60% universities is 7 to 12 periods per week while in 25%, 10% and 5% universities, the work load is 13 to 18, 19 to 24 and upto 6 periods per week respectively.

The lecturer's workload in 43.58%, 17.94%, 10.25%, and 2.56% universities is 13 to 18, 7 to 12, 19 to 24 and upto 6 periods per week respectively.

The workload of part time teachers in first 40% universities is upto 6 periods per week while in other 40% the workload is 7 to 12 periods per week. In 20% universities the work load of part time teachers is 13 to 18 periods per week.

The work load of demonstrators in all the universities is 7 to 12 periods per week.

In Madhya Pradesh, 7 to 12 periods per week the teaching work load of University Professors has been found in 66.66% universities, while in 33.33% universities it is 13 to 18 periods per week only.

In 66.66% and 33.33% universities, the workload of readers is 13 to 18 and 19.24 periods per week respectively.

The workload of lecturers in 75% and 25% universities is 19 to 24 and 13 to 18 periods per week respectively.

Table 4.51
Department Building

Position	*No. of Universities*		*Percentage*	
	India	*M.P.*	*India*	*M.P.*
Separate Building	6	1	15.38	14.28
Located within library	21	4	53.84	57.14
Located with some other department	12	2	30.76	28.57

The Table 4.51 reflects the position of building of department of Library and Information Science Department in the following style. The department of library and

WORKLOAD OF TEACHERS

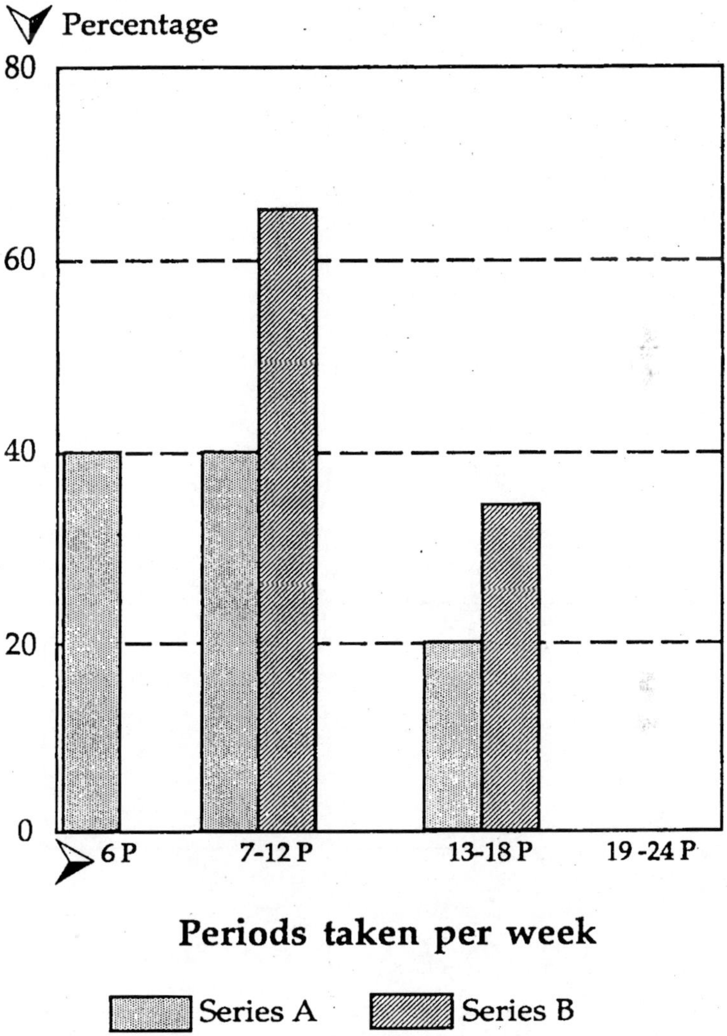

Berlea A - India

Berlea B - M.P.

PART TIME

WORKLOAD OF TEACHERS

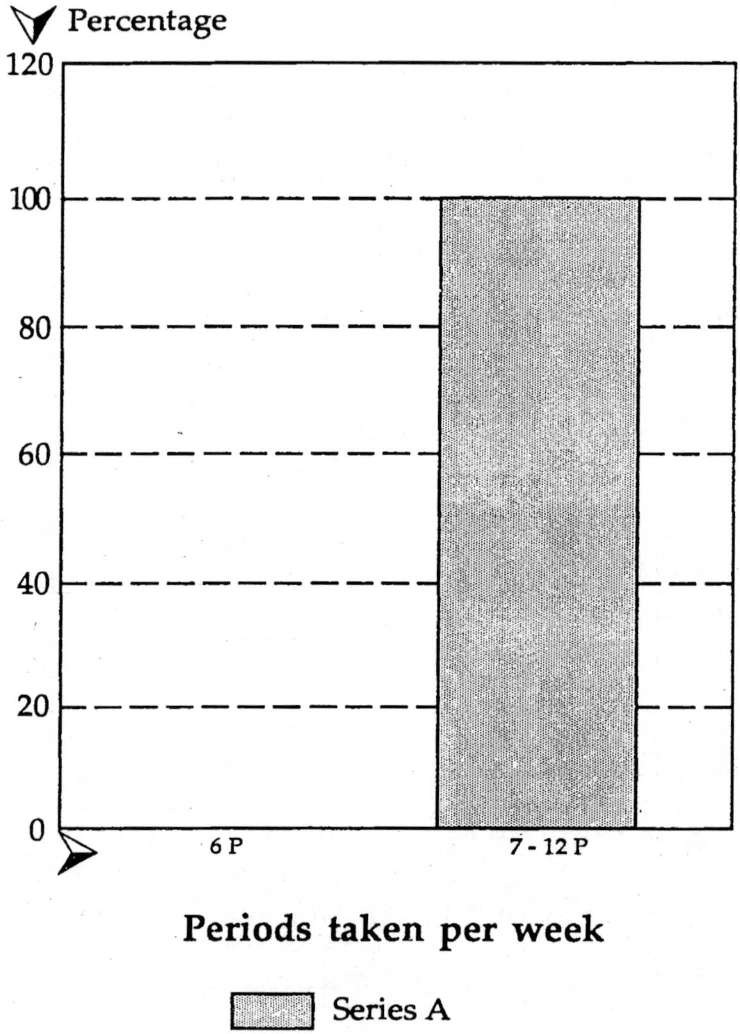

Berlea A - India

DEMONSTRATORS

information science of 53.84% universities are located within the university library building and the department of 30.76% universities are located with some other departments. Only 15.38% universities have separate building for the department.

In Madhya Pradesh, 57.14% departments of library and information science department are located within the university library building. The department of 28.57% universities are located with some other departments. Only 14.28% universities of Madhya Pradesh have separate buildings for the department.

Table 4.52
Accommodation in the Department

Accommodation		*No. of Universities*		*Percentage*	
		India	*M.P.*	*India*	*M.P.*
Lecture room	1-2	32	6	82.05	85.71
	3-4	7	1	17.94	14.28
	5-6	-	-	-	-
Rooms for practical	1	15	2	66.66	28.57
	2	-	-	-	-
Rooms for seminar	1	10	2	25.64	28.57
	2	-	-	-	-
	3	-	-	-	-
Rooms for students	1	11	2	28.20	28.57
	2	-	-	-	-
Rooms for office	1	17	6	43.58	85.71
	2	-	-	-	-
Rooms for head		22	6	56.41	85.71
Room for staff	1	18	2	46.15	28.57
	2	4	2	10.25	58.57
	3	2	-	05.12	-
Other rooms	1	4	1	10.25	14.28
	2	-	1	-	14.28

The Table 4.52 shows that 82.05% universities have accommodation of 1 to 2 rooms for lecture in the department. The accommodation of 3 to 4 lecture rooms exists in 17.94% universities. In 66.66% universities there is one practical room. Rest of the universities do not have any room for practicals, whereas 25.64% universities have one room for seminars.

There is one room for students in 28.20% universities and in 43.58 universities one room for office is available.

There is a room for head in 56.41% universities. As for as room for staff is concerned, 46.15%, 10.25% and 5.12% universities have one, two and three rooms for staff respectively. Only 10.25 universities have one room for other purposes.

In Madhya Pradesh, 85.71% universities have 1 to 2 rooms for lecture and 14.28% universities have 3 to 4 rooms.

There is one practical room in 28.57% universities. One room for seminars in 28.57% universities is available. One room for students exists in 28.57% universities and in 85.71% universities have one room for office. There is one room for heads of the departments in 85.71% universities, 28.57% universities have one room for the staff and in other 28.57% universities two staff rooms are available. In 14.28% universities have another room and other 14.28% universities have two other rooms for other purposes.

Table 4.53
Satisfaction with the Space for the Department

	No. of Universities		*Percentage*	
Satisfaction	*India*	*M.P.*	*India*	*M.P.*
Satisfied	14	3	35.89	42.85
Not satisfied	25	4	64.10	57.14

The Table 4.53 indicates that 35.89% heads of the department are satisfied with space for the department but 64.10% heads are not satisfied.

In Madhya Pradesh, 42.85% heads of the departments are satisfied with the space whereas 57.14% heads are not satisfied with the space.

The Table 4.54 shows that 24.24% heads of the departments feel difficulties in administration when this department located within the university library or with some other departments, but 75.75% heads do not feel any difficulty.

Table 4.54
Difficulties in Administration when Department Located within Library or with Some Other Department

Difficulty	*No. of Universities*		*Percentage*	
	India	*M.P.*	*India*	*M.P.*
Difficulty	8	3	24.24	42.85
No difficulty	25	4	75.75	57.14

In Madhya Pradesh, 42.85% heads feel difficulty while 57.14% heads do not feel any difficulty.

The Table 4.55 shows that 75% heads of the departments feel restrictions in opening hours of the department while 12.5% heads feel inadequacy of space and 12.5% heads feel interference of other administration, because they do not have separate building for the department.

Table 4.55
Types of Difficulties in Administration when not having Own Building

Types of Difficulties	*No. of Universities*		*Percentage*	
	India	*M.P.*	*India*	*M.P.*
Restrictions in opening hrs.	6	2	75	66.66
Inadequacy of space	1	1	12.5	33.33
Interference of other administration	1	-	12.5	-
Other				

In Madhya Pradesh, 66.66%, heads feel restrictions in opening hours of the department whereas 33.33% heads feel inadequacy of space.

Table 4.56
Satisfaction with the Teaching Aids

Satisfaction	*No. of Universities*		*Percentage*	
	India	*M.P.*	*India*	*M.P.*
Most satisfactory	8	2	20.51	28.57
Satisfactory	21	4	53.84	57.14
Not satisfactory	10	1	25.64	14.28

The Table 4.56 reveals that 53.84% heads of the departments are satisfied with the teaching aids in the department, but 25.64% heads are not satisfied whereas 20.51% heads are fully satisfied with the teaching aids.

In Madhya Pradesh, 57.14% heads are satisfied whereas 28.57% and 14.28% heads of the departments are fully satisfied and not satisfied respectively.

Table 4.57
Departmental Library Facility

Facility	*No. of Universities* *India*	*M.P.*	*Percentage* *India*	*M.P.*
Library facility	27	6	69.23	85.71
No library facility	12	1	30.76	14.28

The Table 4.57 denotes that 69.23% departments have library facility while 30.76% departments do not have such facility.

In Madhya Pradesh, 85.71% departments have library facility but 14.28% departments do not have such facility.

Table 4.58
Incharge Department Library

Incharge	*No. of Universities* *India*	*M.P.*	*Percentage* *India*	*M.P.*
Head of the department	10	4	37.03	66.66
Any other teacher	4	2	14.81	33.33
Full time trained persons	13	-	48.14	-
A clerk	Nil	-	-	-

The Table 4.58 shows that 48.14% departments have full time trained person as incharge departmental library. In 37.03 departments, heads of the departments are incharge departmental libraries and 14.81% departments have some teacher incharge of the departmental libraries.

In Madhya Pradesh, heads of the departments are incharge departmental library in 66.66% universities. In 33.33% departments, some other teacher is incharge of the departmental library.

Table 4.59
Procedure for Acquisition of Books and Periodicals for Deptt. Library

Procedure	*No. of Universities*		*Percentage*	
	India	*M.P.*	*India*	*M.P.*
Centralized purchasing by Central Library	18	5	66.66	33.33
Head of the department authorised to purchase	9	1	33.33	16.66
Loaned from Central library	Nil	-	Nil	

The Table 4.59 reflects that where departmental libraries in library and information science exist, 66.66% of them acquire books through centralized purchasing from Central libraries. In 33.33% departmental libraries, heads of the departments are authorised to purchase the books and periodicals.

In Madhya Pradesh, 83.33% departmental libraries acquire the books through centralized purchasing from central libraries. In 16.66%, heads of the departments are authorised to purchase the books and periodicals.

Table 4.60
Annual Average Budget of the Departmental Library

Annual Average Budget	*No. of Universities*		*Percentage*	
	India	*M.P.*	*India*	*M.P.*
Upto Rs. 5,000	12	3	44.44	50
Rs. 50,001 to 7,000	5	-	18.51	-
Rs. 7,001 to 9,000	7	-	25.92	-
Rs. 9,001 to 11,000	1	1	03.70	16.66
Rs, 11,001 to 13,000	1	-	03.70	16.66
Rs, 13,001 to 15,000	1	1	03.70	16.66
More than Rs. 15,000	Nil	1	Nil	16.66

The Table 4.60 indicates that annual average budget of 44.44% departmental libraries is upto Rs. 5,000, 25.92% and 18.51% libraries have the annual average budget of Rs. 7001 to 9,000 and Rs. 5,001 to 7,000 respectively. In 3.70% libraries the budget of Rs. 9,001 to Rs. 11,000 , Rs. 11,001 to Rs. 13,000 and Rs. 13,001 to Rs. 15,000 is there.

ANNUAL BUDGET

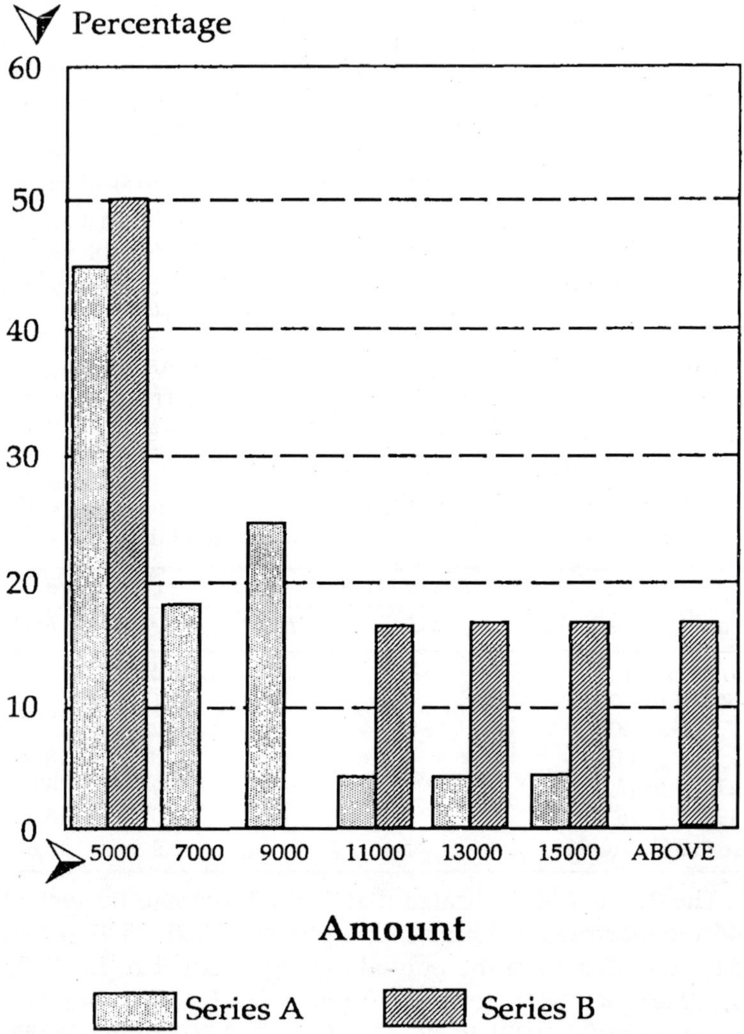

Berlea A - India

Berlea B - M.P.

Deptt. Lib.

In Madhya Pradesh, the annual average budget of 50% departmental libraries are upto Rs. 5,000 and of 16.66% departmental libraries the budget is of Rs. 9,001 to Rs. 11,000, Rs. 11,001 to Rs. 13,000 and Rs. 13,001 to Rs. 15,000 respectively.

Table 4.61
Issue of Books to the Students

	No. of Universities		*Percentage*	
Issue of Books	*India*	*M.P.*	*India*	*M.P.*
Books issued	21	5	77.77	83.33
Books not issued	6	1	22.22	16.66

The Table 4.61 denotes tat 77.77% departmental libraries allow students to get the books issued, whereas 22.22% libraries do not allow.

In Madhya Pradesh, 83.33% departmental libraries allow their students to the books issued but 16.66% libraries do not allow.

Table 4.62(a)
Number of Books Issued to Students

		No. of Universities		*Percentage*	
Class	*No. of Books*	*India*	*M.P.*	*India*	*M.P.*
Undergraduate					
	1 book	1	—	04.76	—
	2 books	18	4	85.71	80
	3 books	Nil	—	Nil	—
	4 books	2	1	09.52	20
Post-graduate					
	2 books	12	—	60	—
	3 books	2	—	10	—
	4 books	6	5	30	100

The Table 4.62(a) shows that in 85.71% departmental libraries, two books are issued to undergraduate *i.e.* B.Lib.I.Sc. students. In 9.52% and 4.76% libraries, the students get four books ad one book respectively.

Table 4.62(b)
Number of Books Issued for the Period

Duration of Period	*No. of Universities*		*Percentage*	
	India	*M.P.*	*India*	*M.P.*
Undergraduate : Less than	—	—	—	—
7 days	3	—	14.28	—
7 days	6	—	28.57	—
15 days	12	5	57.14	100
Post-graduate:				
Less than 7 days	2	—	10	
7 days	6	—	30	—
15 days	12	5	60	100

The 6% departmental libraries allow two books to post-graduate *i.e.* M.Lib.I.Sc. students and in 30% and 10% libraries students get four books and three books from departmental libraries respectively.

In 57.14%, 28.57% and 14.28% departmental libraries allow undergraduate students to get books issued respectively. For the period of 15 days, 7 days and less than 7 days.

The post-graduate students can get the books issued on their name in 60%, 30% and 10% departmental libraries for the period of 15 days, 7 days and less tan 7 days respectively.

In Madhya Pradesh, 80% departmental libraries allow undergraduate students to draw 2 books, while 20% libraries allow them 4 books.

Almost all the libraries allow four books to post-graduate students.

Every departmental library allows both the undergraduate and post-graduate students to keep the books for the period of 15 days.

The Table 4.63 reveals that the collection of books in 51.85% departmental libraries is not sufficient but in 40.74% and 7.40% universities the collection of books are sufficient and most sufficient respectively.

Table 4.63
Collection of Books in the Deptt. Library

	No. of Universities		*Percentage*	
Satisfaction	*India*	*M.P.*	*India*	*M.P.*
Most sufficient	2	1	07.40	16.66
Sufficient	11	3	40.74	50
Not sufficient	14	2	51.85	33.33

In Madhya Pradesh the collection of books in 50%, 33.33% and 16.66% libraries is sufficient, not sufficient and most sufficient respectively.

Table 4.64
Collection of Books and Periodicals in Central Library

	No. of Universities		*Percentage*	
Satisfaction	*India*	*M.P.*	*India*	*M.P.*
Most sufficient	10	2	25.64	28.57
Sufficient	9	4	23.07	57.14
Not sufficient	20	1	51.28	14.28

The Table 4.64 indicates that in 51.28% libraries the collection of books is not sufficient while in 25.64% and 23.7% central libraries have the collection of books and periodicals are most sufficient and sufficient respectively.

In Madhya Pradesh, 57.14% central libraries of the universities have sufficient collection of books and periodicals in library and information science whereas 28.57% and 14.28% central libraries have most sufficient and not sufficient collection respectively.

The Table 4.65 shows that annual tuition fee of M.Lib.I.Sc. course in 45% universities is Rs. 201 to Rs. 300, in 35% universities the annual tuition fee is charged upto Rs. 200. In 5% universities the annual tuition fee is Rs. 301 to Rs. 400, Rs. 501 to 600 and Rs. 700 respectively. But 5% universities charge annual tuition fee more than Rs. 1000.

ANNUAL TUITION FEES

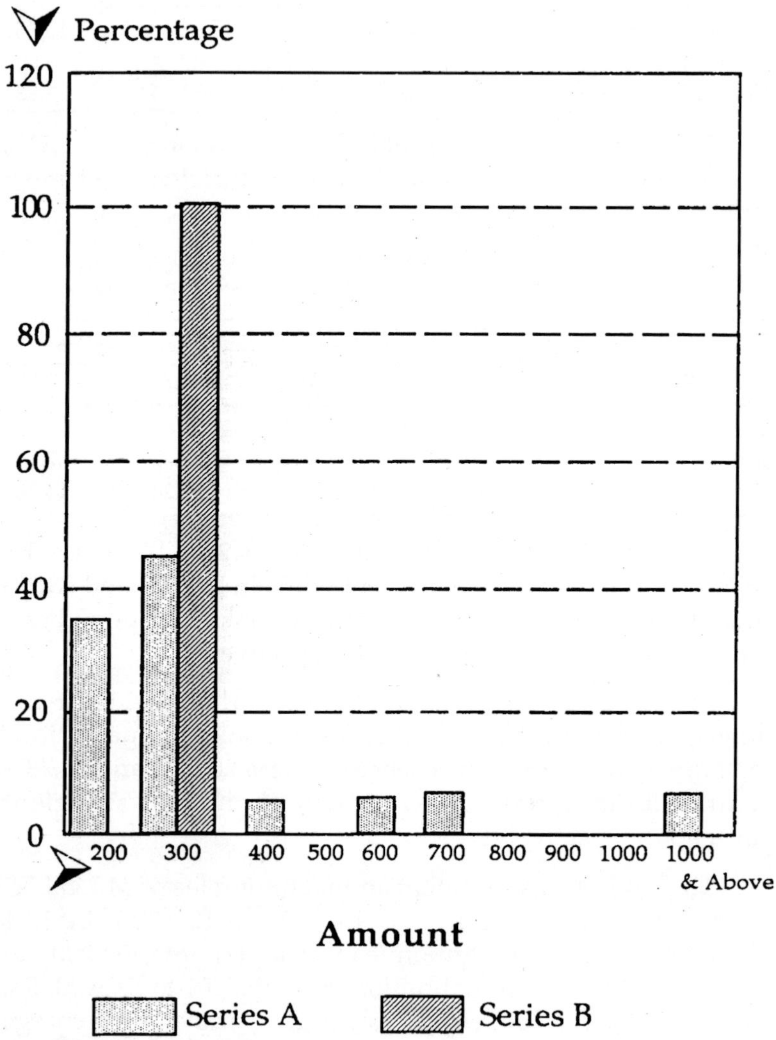

Berlea A - India

Berlea B - M.P.

M.Lib.I.Sc.

ANNUAL TUITION FEES

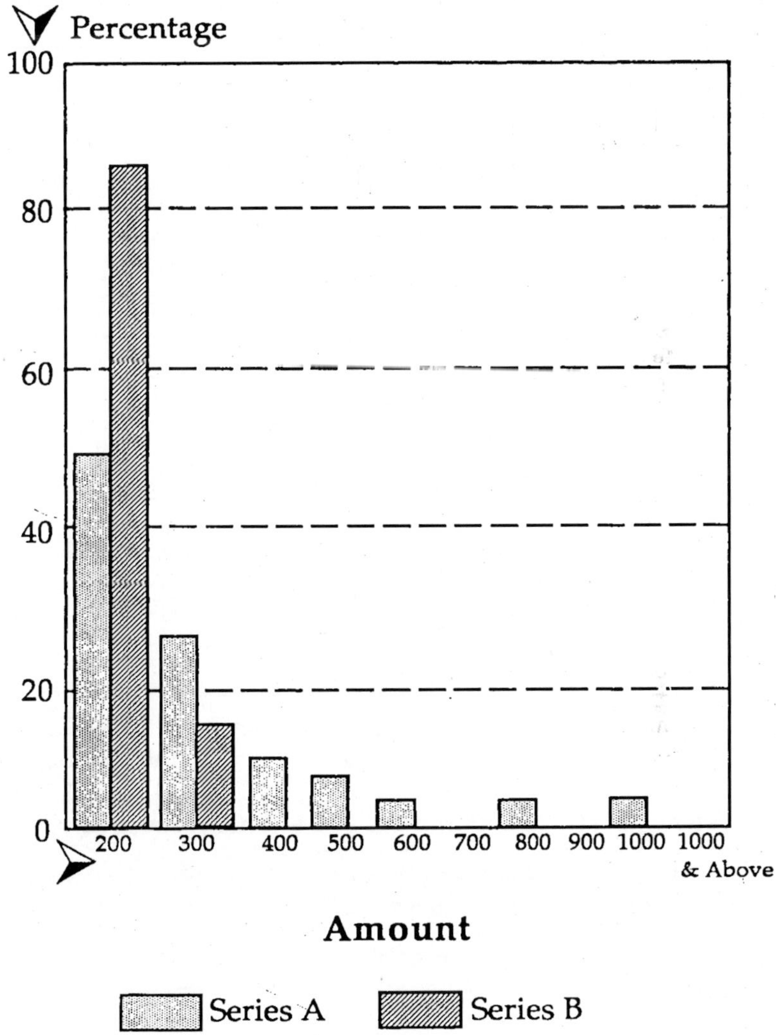

Berlea A - India

Berlea B - M.P.

B.Lib.I.Sc.

Table 4.65
Annual Tuition Fee

	No. of Universities		Percentage	
Amount of Fee	*India*	*M.P.*	*India*	*M.P.*
M.Lib.I.Sc. :				
Upto Rs. 200	7	—	35	
Rs. 201 to 300	9	5	45	100
Rs. 301 to 400	1	—	05	
Rs. 401 to 500	Nil		Nil	
Rs. 501 to 600	1	—	05	
Rs. 601 to 700	1		05	
Rs. 701 to 800	Nil		Nil	
Rs. 801 to 900	Nil		Nil	
Rs. 901 to 1000	Nil	Nil		
More than Rs. 1000	1		05	
B.Lib.I.Sc. :				
Upto Rs. 200	19	6	48.71	85.71
Rs. 201 to 300	11	1	28.20	14.28
Rs. 301 to 400	4		10.25	
Rs. 401 to 500	2		05.12	
Rs. 501 to 600	1		02.56	
Rs. 601 to 700	Nil		Nil	
Rs. 701 to 800	1		02.56	
Rs. 801 to 900	Nil		Nil	
Rs. 901 to 1000	1		02.56	
More than Rs. 1000	Nil		Nil	

The annual tuition fee of B.Lib.I.Sc. course in 48.71%, 28.20%, 10.25%, 5.12%, 2.56%, 2.56% and 2.56% universities is upto Rs. 200, Rs. 201 to 300, Rs. 301 to 400, Rs. 401 to 500, Rs. 501 to 600, Rs. 701 to 800 and Rs. 901 to 1000 respectively.

In Madhya Pradesh, cent per cent universities charge the tuition fee of M.Lib.I.Sc. course Rs. 201 to 300 annually.

The annual tuition fee of B.Lib.I.Sc. student of 85.71% universities is upto Rs. 201 while 14.28% universities charge Rs. 201 to 300 as annual tuition fee for B.Lib.I.Sc. course.

The Table 4.66 indicates that minimum percentage of attendance in the class to appear in the final examination in 76.92% universities is above 75%, while 23.07% universities

FACULTY OF DEPARTMENT

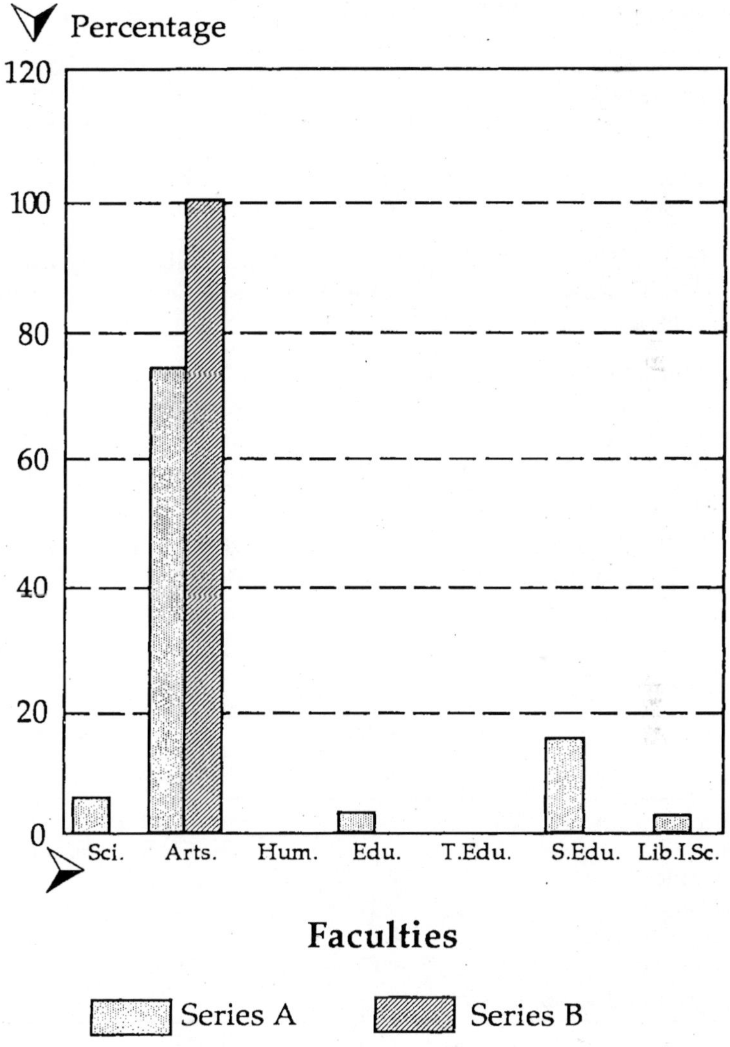

Berlea A - India

Berlea B - M.P.

Lib. & I.Sc.

allow students to appear in the final examination who have above 60% attendance in the class.

Table 4.66
Minimum Percentage of Attendance for Annual Examination

	No. of Universities		*Percentage*	
Percentage of Attendance	*India*	*M.P.*	*India*	*M.P.*
Above 45%	Nil	—	Nil	—
Above 60%	9	2	23.07	28.57
Above 75%	30	5	76.92	71.42

In Madhya Pradesh, 71.42% universities allow only those students to appear in the final examination who have more than 75% attendance in the class.

The Table 4.67 shows that in 74.35% universities the department of library and information science come under the faculty of Arts. In 15.38%, 5.12%, 2.56% universities, it is under the faculty of social science, Science, Education and Library and Information Science.

In Madhya Pradesh, in every university the department of library and information science comes under the faculty of Arts.

Table 4.67
The Faculty of Department of Library and Information Science

	No. of Universities		*Percentage*	
Faculty	*India*	*M.P.*	*India*	*M.P.*
Science	2		05.12	
Arts	29	7	74.35	100
Humanities	Nil		Nil	
Education	1		02.56	
Technical Education	Nil		Nil	
Social Education	6		15.38	
Library and Information Science	1		02.56	

In this way, the analysis of the collected data is completed and in further chapters on this basis, norms are formulated and conclusions are drawn by the researcher from the research study and then few suggestions are made accordingly.

5

NORMS FORMULATED FOR LIBRARY AND INFORMATION SCIENCE EDUCATION FOR UNIVERSITIES OF MADHYA PRADESH

Introduction

In the preceding chapter, an attempt has been made to review the library and information science education in Indian Universities as well as in Madhya Pradesh.

On the basis of this study, the following norms for Library and Information Science Education for the Universities of Madhya Pradesh are formulated. The norms are formulated on the basis of highest percentage of responses to questions by respondants as well as according to the importance of the subject and its salient features.

The courses recommended by U.G.C. panel on Library and Information Science (1982) has also been kept in mind while formulating schemes of papers.

1. Status of head of the department of Library and Information Science Department of a University:

(i) A post-graduate department shall have a university professor;

(ii) An undergraduate department may have a reader.

2. Level of Courses:

University department shall run following courses:

(i) Ph.D. (Library & Information Science);

(ii) M.Phil. (Library & Information Science);

(iii) M.Lib.I.Sc.

(iv) B.Lib.I.Sc.

3. Minimum Qualifications for Admission:

(i) Ph.D. (Library and Information Science)—

A candidate must hold the degree of M.Lib.I.Sc. with minimum 55% marks in aggregate.

(ii) M.Phil. (Library and Information Science)—

A candidate should have a degree of M.Lib.I.Sc. with at least second division or minimum 55% marks in aggregate.

(iii) M.Lib.I.Sc.—

A candidate must possess the degree of B.Lib.I.Sc. with minimum second division.

(iv) B.Lib.I.Sc.—

A candidate must have bachelor's degree in Arts/ Science/Commerce with minimum second division.

(v) Total seats for each course—

(a) Ph.D. (Library and Information Science)—

(1) There should be not limit for the number of seats in the department.

(2) A Supervisor should be allowed to supervise not more than six candidates.

(b) M.Phil.—Ten seats are proposed for M.Phil. in Library and Information Science.

(c) M.Lib.I.Sc.—Twelve seats are proposed at this stage for students.

(d) B.Lib.I.Sc.—Thirty-one to 40 candidates are proposed.

(vi) Reservation of Seats—

(A) Departmental candidates—

(1) At M.Lib.I.Sc. stage 5% of the total seats are proposed.

(2) At B.Lib.I.Sc. stage also five percent seats out of total seats are proposed.

(B) Schedule Caste and Schedule Tribes—

(1) Eleven to fifteen percent seats out of total seats are proposed, at M.Lib.I.Sc.

(2) At B.Lib.I.Sc. also 11 to 15% seats are proposed.

The state government rules may also be applied in this respect.

4. Procedure of Selection of Candidates for Admission:

The criteria for the selection of candidates for admission should be on merit basis. *OR*

An admission test can also be one of the criteria.

The same procedure should be adopted for the departmental candidates also.

5. Following duration for various levels are to be adopted:

(i) M.Phil.—One academic year.

(ii) M.Lib.I.Sc.—One academic year.

(iii) B.Lib.I.Sc.—One academic year.

6. Scheme of Papers:

For papers at different levels following scheme as a NORM is suggested—

Part I—M.Lib.I.Sc.

(1) Universe of knowledge—Its development and structure.

(2) Depth Classification/Advanced Library Classification Theory.

(3) Advanced Library Cataloguing Theory.

(4) Information and Literature source in any one of the following:

(i) The Humanities

(ii) Social Science

(iii) Science

(iv) Medical Science

(v) Engineering and Technology

(vi) Agriculture Sciences etc.

(5) One of the following:

(i) Computer Application in Libraries/Information Centres

(ii) Information Systems and Programmes

(iii) Operations Research and System Analysis.

(6) Advanced Library Organisation and Management of one of the following:

(i) Public Library system

(ii) Academic Library system

(iii) Research and Technical Library System

(iv) Agriculture Library System

(v) Medical Library System

(vi) Engineering and Technological Library System.

(7) Depth Library Classification/Advanced Library Classification (Practice).

(8) Advanced Library Cataloguing (Practice).

Part II— Project Report or Dissertation and Viva.

B.Lib.I.Sc.

(1) Library classification (Theory)

(2) Library classification (Practice)

(3) Library Cataloguing (Theory)

(4) Library Cataloguing (Practice)

(5) Library and Society

(6) Library Organisation and Administration

(7) Reference and Information Sources

(8) Reference and Information Services.

7. Uniformity of Syllabus in the State:

There should be uniformity of syllabus at M.Lib.I.Sc. and B.Lib.I.Sc. levels in the state.

8. Unit System in the Syllabus be followed.

9. Refresher Courses:

The department of Library and Information Science shall organise refresher courses for practicing librarians with the assistance of University Grants Commission, or some other sponsoring agencies either at State or Central levels.

10. Method of examination:

Annual examinations at M.Lib.I.Sc. and B.Lib.I.Sc. levels are to be organised.

11. Maximum marks:

At M.Lib.I.Sc. each paper shall carry 100 marks.

Minimum for First division	60%
For Second division	50%
Minimum for pass	50%

For B.Lib.I.Sc.—Each paper shall carry maximum 100 marks.

Minimum marks for First division	60%
Minimum marks for Second division	50%
Minimum marks for pass	40%

12. Moderation of Annual Question Papers:

The annual question papers shall be moderated by external and internal examiners both.

13. Teaching Hours:

Day hours are to be fixed for teaching to maintain and raise the standard in this respect.

14. Average Number of Hours Per Week:

The average number of hours for M.Lib.I.Sc. and B.Lib.I.Sc. theory papers shall be at least 24 hours.

15. Medium of Instructions:

It shall be English but the regional language can also be used for instruction

16. Seminars:

The department of Library and Information Science should arrange 6 to 7 seminars from time to time.

17. Full Time Teachers:

The department shall have all full time teachers.

18. Strength of full time teachers:

Professor	One
Reader	One
Lecturer	Three

19. Academic Qualification of Teachers:

Educational qualifications laid down by University Grants Commission should be followed.

20. Workload of Teachers:

Professor	7 to 12 periods per week.
Reader	13 to 18 periods per week.
Lecturer	19 to 24 periods per week.

21. Building of the Department:

The department shall have its own independent building. It shall have the following accommodation:

Lecture rooms	2
Room for practical	1
Room for seminar	1
Room for students	1
Room for office	1
Room for head	1
Room for staff	1
Room for Library	1 (big hall).

22. Departmental Library:

The department shall have a library for the use of teachers and students.

The library shall have a trained person.

The library shall have a good collection of books and periodicals (Indian and foreign).

The head of the department shall be authorised to purchase the books for the departmental library.

The students and members of the staff shall have the facility to borrow the books from the library. Atleast two books to B.Lib.I.Sc. students and four books to M.Lib.I.Sc. students shall be allowed to borrow from the library.

23. Annual Tuition Fee:

Following tuition fee is proposed for the various courses in this respect

M.Lib.I.Sc.	Rs. 200 to Rs. 300
B.Lib.I.Sc.	Upto Rs. 200.

24. Minimum Percentage of Attendance:

To appear in the annual examination 75% and above must be compulsory.

25. Faculty of Library and Information Science:

The professional course/subject or discipline may be put under Arts faculty.

6

CONCLUSIONS AND SUGGESTIONS

Introduction

The present research is a study of library and information science education in Indian Universities with a view to formulate norms in Madhya Pradesh. It has been done through a study of selected universities of India and all universities of Madhya Pradesh. The researcher on the basis of the analysis of data has arrived at the following conclusions.

Conclusions

The Study Design

About 65 universities in India are running library and information science education at different levels upto March 1990. Fifty universities out of them were selected for the study and 39 universities out of them have responded. In Madhya Pradesh the following seven Universities are running library and information science education:

1. Dr. Hari Singh Gour Vishwavidyalaya, Sagar,
2. Vikram University, Ujjain,
3. Jiwaji Rao University, Gwalior,
4. Guru Ghasi Das University, Bilaspur,
5. A.P.S. University, Rewa,
6. Rani Durgavati Vishwavidyalaya, Jabalpur,
7. Ravi Shanker University, Raipur.

All of them were selected for the study and hundred percent responded.

Status of the Heads of the Department

It has been concluded that the majority of the departments of library and information in the Universities as well as in Madhya Pradesh are run by professors and readers as heads. In some of the universities, the departments are run either by University librarians or by lecturers as heads of the departments.

Professional Qualifications of the Heads of the Departments

Mostly all the heads of the departments are professionally qualified. They possess master's degree in library and information science. A small number of heads possess bachelor's degree only in library and information science. They should be motivated to improve their professional qualification.

Most of the heads do not possess Ph.D. degree in library and information science. Only some heads (25.64%) possess this degree.

In Madhya Pradesh, majority of the heads of the departments possess M.Lib.I.Sc. degree. As far as Ph.D. in library and information science is concerned, only a few (14.28%) possess Ph.D. degree, which is not a satisfactory position.

Levels of Courses

Ph.D (Library and Information Science) is not common in Indian Universities as well as in Madhya Pradesh. In few Indian universities (41.02%) as well as in Madhya Pradesh (42.85%) Ph.D. (Library and Information Science) is available. Similarly M.Phil. (Library and Information Science) could not be introduced in the universities. A very few Indian universities (2.56%) and universities in Madhya Pradesh (14.28%) could introduce M.Phil. As far as M.Lib.I.Sc. is concerned, it is common in most of the universities. The degree course is run by all the universities.

Minimum Qualification for Admission

M.Lib.I.Sc. degree with second division is the minimum

qualification for the registration in Ph.D. (Library and Information Science) in most of the Indian Universities as well as in Madhya Pradesh some universities (25%) have prescribed B.Lib.I.Sc. degree with second division and M.Lib.I.Sc. degree with second division for Ph.D. registration.

The most of the Indian Universities have uniformity in minimum qualification for admission to M.Lib.I.Sc. and B.Lib.I.Sc. course. The candidates must have bachelor's degree in Library and Information Science with second division for the admission to M.Lib.I.Sc. course. A bachelor's degree in Arts/Science/Commerce with second division is the minimum qualification for admission to B.Lib.I.Sc. course in most of the Indian Universities including those in Madhya Pradesh.

Total Seats

Ph.D. (Library and Information Science)—No uniformity has been found regarding number of candidates with each supervisor. In some Universities (31.25%), 6 candidates per supervisor are allowed. In 25% universities, 8 to 10 candidates per supervisor are allowed. In rest of the universities, there is no limit of candidates per supervisor. It is not good in the interest of the candidates. A supervisor can not spare sufficient time to supervise unlimited candidates. There must be some limit and on the basis of average, this study revealed that a supervisor can supervise six candidates efficiently.

M.Lib.I.Sc.—The Indian Universities could not maintain the uniformity in number of seats in M.Lib.I.Sc. course. Some universities (30%) have 8 to 10 seats. Other universities (20%) have 5 to 7 and 14 to 16 seats. A few universities have 11 to 13 and 17 to 20 seats respectively.

On averaging it is found that 12 is the appropriate number of seats for M.Lib.I.Sc. course.

B.Lib.I.Sc.—Twenty one to 30 seats in B.Lib.I.Sc. course are found in many of the universities. Some universities (17.94%, 15.38% and 10.25%) have 31 to 40, 10 to 20 and 41 to 50 seats respectively. A few universities (2.56%) have 61 to 70 seats.

On averaging 31 to 40 seats are an ideal number for this course. The increase in number of seats will not only reduce the standard of the professional course but it will give rise to unemployment.

Reservation of Seats

Mostly, all universities have reservation of seats for different categories.

Departmental Candidates: M.Lib.I.Sc.

Most of the universities have seats for departmental candidates. They have kept 5%, 6%, to 10%, 31% to 35%, 16% to 20% and 21% to 25% seats for departmental candidates.

Departmental Candidates: B.Lib.I.Sc.

Most of the universities (40% and 30%) have upto 5% and 6% to 10% seats respectively. Some universities have a very large number of seats for departmental candidates. They have 31% to 35% and 46% to 50% seats.

It is agreed that the departmental candidates should have reservation of seats in M.Lib.I.Sc. and B.Lib.I.Sc. course but it should not be very large percentage. A quota of 5% seats is sufficient for departmental candidates to improve their professional qualifications.

Scheduled Caste and Scheduled Tribes Candidates: M.Lib.I.Sc. and B.Lib.I.Sc.

There is no uniformity in number of seats reserved for scheduled caste and scheduled tribes in Indian universities including those in Madhya Pradesh. Some universities (40% and 30%) have 11% to 15% and 31% to 35% seats of them in M.Lib.I.Sc. course. Other universities have 26% to 30% and 36% to 40% seats. In B.Lib.I.Sc. course some universities (37% and 25%) have 11% to 15% and 16% to 25% seats. The other universities have 31% to 35%, 26% to 30%, 36% to 40% and 21 to 25% seats.

In Madhya Pradesh most of the Universities have 16% to 20% seats for SC/ST candidates in M.Lib.I.Sc. course. In B.Lib.I.Sc. course mostly universities (42.85% and 28.57%) have

31% to 35% and 16% to 20% seats for SC/ST. The rest of the universities have no seats for them.

A university in this respect is needed.

Procedure of Selection of Candidates

The procedure of selection of candidates to various courses is different in various Indian Universities. Some Universities (35.89%, 25.64% and 20.51%) select the candidates on merit, merit-cum-interview and written-cum-interview basis respectively. A few universities (15.38% and 2.56%) select them on merit-cum-test basis and written test basis respectively.

In Madhya Pradesh all the universities select them on merit-cum-interview basis except a few universities. They select them on merit and merit-cum-test basis.

Duration of Courses

M.Lib.I.Sc.—Most of the universities in India including those in Madhya Pradesh have one academic year for this course. Some universities have 12, 15 and 14 months' course.

B.Lib.I.Sc.—Most of the Indian Universities including the universities of Madhya Pradesh, have one academic year course. A few universities have 12 months and 9 months course.

Library Science Course through Correspondence

Most of the universities do not run library science course through correspondence. Only a few universities (12.82%) run correspondence course Library Science courses through correspondence should be discouraged because candidates do not get through practical knowledge of library classification, library cataloguing and technical processing etc.

Contents of Courses :

M.Lib.I.Sc. 30 papers are taught at M.Lib.I.Sc. level in different Indian Universities. The details of the papers including practice dissertation and viva are concluded below.

The Universe of Knowledge—Its development and structure, the depth classification/advance library classification and advanced library cataloguing theory and practice are common in most of the Indian universities. In Madhya Pradesh, these papers are common in all the universities.

Advanced reference service is not taught as an independent paper in universities. It is taught in some universities (25%) with bibliography of literature in social science or natural science or applied science or humanities. It is not taught in most of the universities.

Reference service with documentation is taught in a few (5%) universities.

In Madhya Pradesh, reference service is taught with bibliography of literature in most (60%) of the universities.

Documentation as an independent paper is not very common. It is taught in a few (5%) universities. It is taught in some universities with reference service as stated above but in Madhya Pradesh it is taught with information retrieval in most of the universities.

Fundamentals of information science is an important papers but as an inpedendent paper, it is taught in some (40%) universities. In some (25%) universities, it is taught under the little information storage retrieval. In other universities, information systems and programming, information control techniques, information and communication, planning of information systems, information transfer and dissemination papers are taught but the number of these universities is very small. In Madhya Pradesh, information storage and information retrieval as an independent paper is common in some (40%) universities but it is taught with documentation in most of the other universities.

Computers and application could not be introduced in most of the universities. It is taught in a few (15%) universities only. Similarly, it is introduced in some (20%) universities of Madhya Pradesh.

Research methodology is not common in most of the universities. Only some (25%) universities introduced it as an independent paper. A few universities introduced it with information service and system analysis. In Madhya Pradesh none of the universities introduced it.

Organization of special material has been introduced in a few (5%) universities. Advanced library organization and management of either public libraries or academic libraries or special libraries is common in most of the (65%) universities. It is also common in all the universities of Madhya Pradesh.

Measurement and Evaluation will take time to get popularity. It is popular in a few (10%) universities. Similarly, comparative librarianship part I and II and International librarianship are common in a few (10% and 20%) universities respectively.

System analysis is not an independent paper in any university. It is taught in a few universities with library management or statistical methods. Advanced technical processing theory and practice have been introduced in a few (10%) universities. These papers have not been introduced in any of the universities in Madhya Pradesh.

Dissertation and viva are common in the Indian Universities including the Universities of Madhya Pradesh.

B.Lib.I.Sc.—Twenty-five papers are taught in different Indian universities at B.Lib.I.Sc. level whereas in Madhya Pradesh, only 13 papers are taught in different universities. The details of the papers taught in different universities are given below:

Library Classification (theory and practice) and Library Cataloguing (theory and practice) is common in all the Indian Universities including the Universities of Madhya Pradesh. There is no disparity in these papers.

Library and Society is common in most of the universities (63.23%), but in Madhya Pradesh it is common in some universities (42.85%) only.

Library organization and administration is taught in many universities (41.02%), Library organization is taught in some Universities (23.07%) as a separate paper. Library management is taught in a few (2.56%) universities with library systems. Library organization and administration is taught in a few universities of Madhya Pradesh but it is taught under the titles library organization old library management in most of the universities.

Some Indian universities (33.33%) teach book selection, bibliography and reference service. In Madhya Pradesh, it is common in some (42.85%) universities. Most of the universities (57.14%) do not teach this paper.

Reference service as a separate paper has been kept in the syllabus of a few (20.51%) Indian Universities. Majority of the universities have kept it with information service or information sources.

History of books and printing, bibliography and literature in a specialized field, community and society, comparative librarianship, library system, General knowledge, physical bibliography, reprography and book trade are taught in a few universities. Similarly information science is taught in a few universities. Some universities have introduced viva at B.Lib.I.Sc. level but most of the Indian universities (66.66%) including those of M.P. did not feel it necessary (Table 4.19).

In Madhya Pradesh, Information Science is very popular in majority of the universities (71.42%) but it is taught with documentation.

Uniformity of Syllabus in the State

Most of the universities including universities of Madhya Pradesh do not have uniformity in syllabus at M.Lib.I.Sc. and B.Lib.I.Sc. level.

Unit System in the Syllabus

Unit system has not been added in the syllabus in most of the Indian universities including those in Madhya Pradesh.

Need for Organising Some Refresher Courses for Practicing Librarians

Most of the heads of the Department of Indian Universities feel the need for organizing some refresher courses for practicing librarians. The heads of the departments of universities of Madhya Pradesh can not deny this fact. Most of the heads of the departments, including Madhya Pradesh have suggested that departments of library and information science should arrange these refresher courses. Some heads have suggested the names of U.G.C., Library Associates, ICSSR and CSIR to conduct refresher courses (Table 4.23 and 4.24).

System of Examination

It is revealed that most of the Indian Universities including those in Madhya Pradesh follow annual examination system at M.Lib.I.Sc. and B.Lib.I.Sc. levels. A few universities follow semester system for evaluating the M.Lib.I.Sc. and B.Lib.I.Sc. students.

Maximum and Minimum Marks: M.Lib.I.Sc.

Almost in all the Indian Universities as well as in the universities of Madhya Pradesh, total 800 marks for M.Lib.I.Sc. examination are fixed. First division is awarded on 60% marks in all the universities. Second division is awarded on 50% marks in most of the universities. A few universities award second division on 48% and 45% marks. In most of the universities, 50% marks are minimum for passing the examination.

In most of the universities of M.P. maximum 800 marks have been fixed at M.Lib.I.Sc. level. Some universities have fixed 900 maximum marks, 50% marks for second division are common in all the universities but there is a variation in fixing minimum pass marks. Most of the universities have fixed 50% marks whereas some universities have fixed 40% pass marks for M.Lib.I.Sc. examination (Table 4.27).

B.Lib.I.Sc.

In most of the Indian universities of Madhya Pradesh total 800 marks have fixed for B.Lib.I.Sc. examination. Some universities have allotted 850, 900, 950 and 1,000 maximum marks.

There is no disparity in the percentage of first division. All the universities award first division on 60% marks.

Most of the universities including those in Madhya Pradesh allot second division on 50% marks. A few universities allot second division on 48% and 45% marks. Fourty percent marks are common in most of the universities including those of Madhya Pradesh at B.Lib.I.Sc. level (Table 4.28).

Moderation of Question Papers

Question papers are moderated in most of the universities. In majority of the universities, the annual question papers are moderated by external and internal experts. But in some cases, they get the moderation done by external experts only. A few universities do not feel the necessity of moderation of question papers, while in Madhya Pradesh, less than half of the Universities do not have system of moderation of question papers at all. In half of the universities, where question papers are moderated, moderation work is done by external and internal expert and in other half of the universities, the question papers are moderated by external experts only.

Research Facility

The research facility for Ph.D. in library and information science, is not available in most of the universities. It is available in some universities (35.89%). Similarly in Madhya Pradesh research facility is available in some universities (42.85%). Most of the universities could not provide the research facility because they do not have post graduation and qualified research supervisors.

Ph.D. Degree Awarded and Research in Progress

Ph.D. in library and information science is not very common like Ph.Ds in other disciplines. One to three Ph.D. degree were awarded in some universities (28.57%). A few universities (14.28%) awarded four to six degrees. It can be concluded that no Ph.D. degree was awarded in many Indian universities. In Madhya Pradesh, a few universities (14.28%) awarded one to three Ph.D. degrees. Most of the universities could not award any Ph.D. in library and information science.

Now Ph.D. in Library and Information Science has gained progress in most of the universities. One to six Ph.Ds are in progress in some universities (21.42). Thirteen to eighteen Ph.Ds are in progress in other universities (21.42%). Seven to twelve Ph.Ds are in progress in a few universities (14.28%).

In Madhya Pradesh, not many Ph.Ds have been awarded in this discipline, only one to three Ph.D. degrees have been awarded in a few universities (14.28%). No Ph.D. in Library and Information Science has been awarded in most of the universities; but it is in progress. One to six researches are in progress in some universities (28.57%). Seven to twelve researches are in progress in a few universities (14.28%).

Area of Researches Completed and Research in Progress

About 55 researches have been completed or in progress in the field of documentation and information science, academic library, library administration, library organization, library classification and library cataloguing.

In Madhya Pradesh, about 20 researches have been completed or in progress in the field of documentation and information science, academic library, library administration, library classification, library cataloguing and public library. It is concluded that mostly researches completed or in progress are in the field of documentation and information science. Some researches are completed or in progress in the field of academic library and library administration. A few researches are completed or in progress in the field of library classification and library cataloguing. Reference service has been neglected so far (Table 4.33).

Teaching Hours

The teaching hours in most of the universities including those in Madhya Pradesh are day hours. A few universities have morning and evening classes.

Average Number of Hours Per Week: M.Lib.I.Sc.

Mostly universities have 19 to 24 hours per week. Some universities have 25 to 30 and 12 to 18 hours. A few universities have 31 to 36 hours per week for M.Lib.I.Sc. teaching.

B.Lib.I.Sc.

Most of the universities have 19 to 24 hours per week for B.Lib.I.Sc. teaching. Some Universities have 25 to 30 hours. A few universities have 12 to 18, 31 to 36, 37 to 42 and 43 to 48 hours per week.

On an average 19 to 24 hours are allotted per week in a majority of the universities (80%) for M.Lib.I.Sc. teaching. A few universities have 25 to 30 hours.

The average number of hours, per week for B.Lib.I.Sc. is 19 to 24 in many universities (57.14%). Some Universities have 31 to 36 and 43 to 48 hours per week. It is concluded that average 19 to 24 hours are common in most of the universities for M.Lib.I.Sc. and B.Lib.I.Sc. teaching.

Methods of Teaching

The lecture method has been given highest weightage in teaching library and information science at M.Lib.I.Sc. and B.Lib.I.Sc. level. Second and third weightage has been given to seminar and tutorial methods respectively. Practical work has been given fourth weightage. No weightage has been give to discussion, observation and apprenticeship. In fact, the students should be instructed through lectures, seminars, classroom discussions, practical work, field trips, projects and case studies.

Medium of Instruction

As all the related literature with library and information science, is mostly available in English, the medium of instruction is also English in most of the universities. It is observed that in some of the universities, regional languages are also adopted alongwith English. English plus Hindi and English plus Gujrati are used in some state universities. In a few universities, Punjabi is used with English and in some Hindi speaking areas, purely Hindi Language is used as medium of instruction. It is concluded that English language is a popular medium of instruction in library and information science.

Madhya Pradesh being Hindi speaking area, English is

used in most of the universities with Hindi, purely English is used in a few universities (14.28%). In similar number of universities, purely Hindi is used as medium of instruction.

Seminars

Many departments of library and information science arranged seminars from time to time though they could arrange five seminars only. A few universities could arrange seminars 11 to 15 or more than that. Some universities could not arrange any seminar. In Madhya Pradesh, a few universities arranged seminars 6 to 10 and 16 to 20 seminars (Table 4.41 and 4.42)

Full Time Teachers

Most of the universities have full time teachers in the department of library and information science. Only some universities (25.64%) do not have full time teachers. The similar position is seen in Madhya Pradesh.

Strength of Full Time Teachers

There are total 106 full time teachers. The strength of teachers in different cadre is given below:

Udiversity Professor : Most of the universities do not have professors. Some of the Universities (34.48%) have one Professor. In Madhya Pradesh except some, most of the universities have professors.

Rea ers: Majority of Indian Universities have readers. Most of them have one reader. A few universities (13.79%) and (6.89%) have two and three readers. Some of the universities (31.03%) do not have any reader.

In Madhya Pradesh majority of the universities have readers. Fifty percent universities have one reader. Twenty-five percent universities have two readers and others do not have any readers.

Lecturers: Two lecturers are found in many universities (44.82%). Some universities have one, three, four and five lecturers. The post of demonstrator is rarely found.

In Madhya Pradesh, one lecturer is found in majority of

universities. Three lecturers are found in some of the universities (25%).

Academic Qualification of the Teachers

Maximum teachers possess post-graduate degree in Arts/ Science/Commerce. A few teachers possess bachelor's degree in Arts/Science/Commerce.

Most of the teachers (66.98%) possess post-graduate degree in library and information science. Other teachers (33.01%) have bachelor's degree only in library and information science.

A few teachers (19.81%) possess doctorate degree in library and information science. A few teachers possess M.Phil (Library and Information Science). A few teachers possess doctorate degree in other than library and information science.

In Madhya Predesh, all the teachers possess post-graduate degree in Arts/Science/Commerce as well as degree in library and information science. So far as Ph.D. in Library and Information Science is concerned, a few teachers (16.66%) possess the degree. A few teachers (8.33%) possess Ph.D. in the subject other than library and information science.

Teacher's Guiding Research

In most of the universities (64.10%) the research guides are not available. Only in some universities (17.94%, 10.25% and 7.69%), one, two or three teachers are available guiding research work at Ph.D. level.

In Madhya Pradesh, the availability of research guides is comparatively in better position. In some universities (28.57%) one guide is available. In other universities (28.57%) two teachers are available guiding research work. In rest of the universities (42.85%), no guide is available.

Research Fellowship in Library and Information Science

Research fellowship was awarded in a few universities (10.25%). It could not be awarded in most of the universities including those in Madhya Pradesh.

Number of Part-Time Teachers

Some universities (25.64%) do not have full time teachers and teaching work is assigned to part-time teachers. In half of these universities, the number of part time teachers is three to four. Some of the universities have one to two part time teachers. A few universities have five to six part time teachers. In Madhya Pradesh some universities (42.85%) have three to four part time teachers.

Payment of Honorarium to Part Time Teachers

The payment of honorarium of part time teachers is very poor in all the universities. The services of part time teachers are under exploitation. Most of the universities pay Rs. 250 to Rs. 750 per month. A few universities pay Rs. 751 to Rs. 1,000 and Rs. 1001 to Rs. 1250 per month. Some of the universities pay Rs. 15, Rs. 25 and Rs. 40 per lecture.

In Madhya Pradesh also, very poor honorarium is paid to part time teachers. Majority of the universities pay Rs. 251 to Rs. 500 per month. Some universities pay up to Rs. 250 per month. (Table 4.48 and Table 4.49).

Workload of Teachers

The workload of professors in most of the universities including those in Madhya Pradesh is seven to twelve periods per week. In some universities, it is thirteen to eighteen and in some other universities, it is upto six periods per week only which is very light workload.

Rea ers: In most of the universities, the workload of readers, is seven to twelve periods per week. In some universities (25% and 10%), it is thirteen to eighteen and nineteen to twenty-four periods per week. In Madhya Pradesh thirteen to eighteen and nineteen to twenty four periods per week are found in most of the universities.

Lecturers: There is much variation in work load of lecturers in different univerisites. Thirteen to eighteen and seven to twelve periods are generally found in most of the universities. Nineteen to twenty four periods per week are assigned in some universities. A few universities have assigned upto six periods per week which is not justified as per U.G.C. guide lines.

In Madhya Pradesh, U.G.C. guide lines have been followed to a great extent. Most of the universities (75%) have assigned nineteen to twenty-four periods per week to lecturers. In some of the universities (25%), thirteen to eighteen periods per week are assigned to lecturers.

Part Time Teacher

It seems that the work load of part time teachers depends upon the availability of number of part time teachers. It is, therefore, in some of the universities (40%), only upto six periods have been assigned. In some other universities (40%), seven to twelve periods per week are assigned to them. Only in a few universities, their workload is thirteen to eighteen periods per week.

Demodstrator : All the universities have assigned seven to twelve periods per week to them (Table 4.50).

Building of the Department

It is concluded that majority of universities including those in Madhya Pradesh, do not have their own building. In most of the universities, the departments are located within the university library building. In some universities, the departments are located in the building of some other department. A few universities have their own building. In Madhya Pradesh also, a few universities have the separate building for the department of library and information science. In other universities, the department is located within the library of with some other department (Table 4.51).

Accommodation in the Department

Mostly universities (82.05%) including those in Madhya Pradesh have one to two lecture rooms. Most of the departments have one room for practical. A few departments have a room for seminars. Most of the departments have rooms for staff and heads of the departments (Table 4.52).

Satisfaction with Space

Most of the heads of the departments are not satisfied with the space for the department. They need more space. Some heads have shown their satisfaction with the present condition. The heads of the departments of Madhya Pradesh also are not satisfied with the space which they utilize (Table 4.53).

Teaching Aids

Most of the departments of Indian Universities including those in Madhya Pradesh, have satisfactory teaching aids. Some departments do not have satisfactory teaching aids.

Departmental Library Facility

Most of the universities have departmental libraries in library and information science. Only a few universities do not have departmental libraries. The universities should establish departmental libraries in these departments.

In most of the universities, the books and periodicals are acquired through centralized purchasing by University Central Libraries. In some universities, heads of the departments are authorized to purchase the books and periodicals for their departmental libraries and so is the case with Madhya Pradesh. In most of the universities, the books and periodicals are acquired through centralized purchasing. In a few universities, the heads of the departments are authorized for direct purchasing.

Annual Average Budget of the Departmental Libraries

Keeping in view the increasing cost of books and periodicals, the average annual budget is not sufficient to meet the requirements of the departmental libraries. Most of the departmental libraries have an average annual budget of Rs. 5000 to Rs. 9000. A few departmental libraries have an average budget of Rs. 9001 to Rs. 15000. So is the case with the Universities of Madhya Pradesh.

Number of Books Loaned to Students

Loan facility of books to students is provided in a majority of departmental libraries. A few departmental libraries (22.22%) do not provide this facility.

In most of the libraries, two and four books are loaned to B.Lib.I.Sc. and M.Lib.I.Sc. students. A few departmental libraries allow three or four books to them. In most of the libraries the books are loaned to them for the period of fifteen days. A few libraries allow them for a period of seven days.

In Madhya Pradesh, most of the departmental libraries allow two books to B.Lib.I.Sc. students for a period of fifteen days. Four books are loaned to M.Lib.I.Sc. students for a period of fifteen days in all the departmental libraries (Table 4.61 and 4.62(a) and 4.62(b)).

Collection of Books in the Departmental Libraries

Most of the departmental libraries do not have sufficient collection of books. Some universities have sufficient collection. A few universities (7.40%) have most sufficient collection of books in departmental libraries. In Madhya Pradesh, many universities have sufficient collection of books. It is found that some universities do not have sufficient collection while few universities have most sufficient collection in departmental libraries (Table. 4.63).

Collection of Books and Periodicals in Central Library

Collection of books and periodicals in Central libraries is not sufficient in most of the universities. Only in some universities it is sufficient or more than sufficient.

So far as Madhya Pradesh is concerned, most of the Central libraries of universities have sufficient collection of books and periodicals in library and information science. But some have a very good collection of books and periodicals. Only a few universities do not have sufficient collection of books and periodicals (Table 4.64).

Annual Tuition Fee

M.Lib.I.Sc.—There is no uniformity in tuition fees. Some universities (45%) charge Rs. 201 to Rs. 300 per annum. Some Universities (35%) charge upto Rs. 200. A few universities (5%) charge Rs. 301 to Rs. 400, Rs. 501 to Rs. 600 and Rs. 601 to Rs. 700 per annum. Few Universities (5%) charge more than Rs. 1000 per annum.

B.Lib.I.Sc.—Some universities (48.71%) charge upto Rs. 200/- per annum. Some of the universities (28.20%, 10.25% and 5.12%) charge Rs. 201 to Rs. 300, Rs. 301 to Rs. 400 and Rs. 401 to Rs. 500 per annum respectively. Few universities chare Rs. 501 to Rs. 600, Rs. 701 to Rs. 800 and Rs. 901 to Rs. 1000 per annum.

In Madhya Pradesh, mostly all the universities charge up to Rs. 300 per annum for M.Lib.I.Sc. course upto Rs. 200 per annum for B.Lib.I.Sc. course (Table 4.65).

Minimum Percentage of Attendance to Appear at the Examinations

The conclusion in this respect is that there is uniformity in minimum percentage of attendance to appear at the examination almost in all the Indian universities as well as in the universities of Madhya Pradesh. They allow the students to appear at the examinations who have attended 75% lectures out of total lectures. A few universities allow them on 60% attendance.

Faculty of Library and Information Science

In most of the universities (74.35%), the department of library and information science comes under the faculty of arts. In a few universities it comes under the faculty of social science, science education and library and information science.

Norms Formulated for Library and Information Science Education in the Universities of Madhya Pradesh

The norms have been formulated for the following aspects:

1. Level of Causes.
2. Number of Seats for Ph.D., M.Lib.I.Sc. and B.Lib.I.Sc.
3. Criteria of selection of candidates.
4. Duration of courses.
5. Schemes of Papers.
6. Maximum and Minimum Marks.
7. Teaching Hours and Number of Hours.

8. Number of Full Time Teachers.
9. Academic Qualification of the Teachers.
10. Workload of Teachers.
11. Department Building.
12. Departmental Library.
13. Annual Tuition Fee.
14. Minimum Percentage of Attendance.
15. Faculty of Library and Information Science.

Discussion of Results

To verify the reliability, validity and significance of the results obtained by the researcher in this study, it is essential as well as useful to test the obtained results in the light of studies occurred/made in India and abroad.

In the field of research/Ph.D. the result of this study is that very few universities in India and particularly in Madhya Pradesh have facility and motivation for research/Ph.D. work. So there is a need to motivate and advance and research in Library Science and Information Science. Danton (1959) concluded in his study the problems faced by scholars during their Ph.D. Harlow (1968) recognised the importance of Ph.D. at the time of selection for employment. Marco (1967) in his study found Library science as a subject for doctorate standard. Dennis and Hauses (1972) also concluded the need and importance of Ph.D. in the sphere of Library Science. Kapoor (1968) in his study found the students' interest in the field of research in Library and Information Science.

Regarding the reservation of seats in Library and Information Science, almost all the universities in India as well as of Madhya Pradesh have provided reservation to Schedule Caste/Schedule Tribe and backward class in some definite proportion. Mitra (1991) has observed the reservation provision in Indian constitution as well as in the light of judicial decision in respect of admission to Higher Academic Courses.

So far as the contents of all the levels in Library and

Information Science are converted, the conclusion of this study shows that there is no uniformity in respect of contents/ courses in Library and Information Science among Indian and Madhya Pradesh universities. Some foreign and Indian studies also reveal no uniformity in contents of Library Science. Grotzinger (1971) in his study, found the absence of field study/experience in the curriculum. Singh (1967) also found that Bombay School is the only school which holds Practical examination in this field. Kapoor and Kaur (1980) also found in their study the absence of uniformity in Library Science course.

No uniformity in the procedure of selection of candidates to various courses in Indian Universities including Universities of Madhya Pradesh is found in this study. Marco (1967) also found a little uniformity in entrance requirement.

Most of the universities have full time teachers but the strength of full time teachers in Indian universities is not sufficient. Mostly universities do not have professors. Similarly most of the universities have only one reader and two lecturers only. William (1969) also found in his study that the teaching staff at the institute of Librarianship included one one Nigerian lecturer, the other three members of the school's faculty being drawn from outside, Nigeria. Kapoor and Ravinder Kaur (1980) concluded in this study that most of the universities did not have full time teaching staff. But now the position regarding full time teaching staff has improved. Mangla (1990) finds in his study that number of full time teachers in library schools in the country is estimated at 250 with 30 professors, 80 readers and 140 lecturers. Mangla further finds that 90% of library schools have full time teachers and heads and others still function under the respective university librarians who have the additional responsibility for the schools.

It is concluded in this study that lecture method is generally used in most of the universities. Seminar and tutorial methods are given second and third weightage. Practical method has been given fourth method. Chapman (1970) also found in his study of British library schools that lecture method was apparently extensively used in all the schools. Grotzinger (1971) concluded in the study of American schools that practical work was not appropriate in graduate schools.

Annual examination system has been found in majority of the Indian Universities at M.Lib.I.Sc. and B.Lib.I.Sc. levels. A very few universities follow semester system. Singh (1967) also finds that pattern of examination in almost all the schools is the same. Only in a few schools some difference is found in mode of papers and pattern of examination.

In this study, it is found that there are theory paper in each subject and practical examination in library classification and cataloguing. Very few Universities conduct practical examination in reference service. Each paper carries 100 marks. Singh (1967) also finds almost the same. He further finds that Bombay School perhaps is the only school which conducts the practical examination in reference service. The practical examination in library classification and cataloguing is performed by question papers in all the schools except Banaras and Rajasthan schools. In these schools the practical examination in both the subjects is performed by the supply of actual books.

It has been found that U.G.C. has laid down Ph.D. as essential qualification for the post of Professors and Readers. Lecturers are also given preferences who possess the degree of Ph.D. in the subject. Harlow (1968) also finds in his study that selection committees are likely to the impressed by an applicant who posses Ph.D. Certainly the indications are that the doctorate is an useful adjunct for those seeking professional advancement.

In this study, it has been found that there is no uniformity so far as minimum qualification is concerned for the registration in Ph.D. Similarly, the number of scholarships the subject is very less. There is a remarkable lack of uniformity in the doctorate programmes now being offered in the United States. Marco (1967) could find little uniformity in entrance requirement, methods of study (or in the qualifications which are awarded). A serious threat to the development of doctoral study in librarianship in America has come with the possible reduction in the number of fellowships being awarded by the federal government.

It is found in this study that mostly, researches completed and in progress are in the field of documentation and information science. After documentation and information science, academic library and library administration have been given next importance for research. A very few researches have been completed in the field of library classification, library cataloguing. Reference Service has been totally neglected. The popularity of library history as a subject for doctoral investigation was confirmed by Danton (1959) in his study. Kapoor (1968) finds in his study of education for librarianship in Indian universities that majority of students are interested in research in classification. Thirty-five percent are interested in cataloguing, 35% in reference service, 20% are interested in other subjects. It is encouraging to see that 'automation' has been given a thought by these future librarians. Devarajan (1988) surveyed, analysed and provided the recent trends at the post-graduate level researches in library science conducted in India in the first half of 1980's. Tejomurthy (1988) studies the growth of master of library and information Science dissertations of Vikram University Ujjain from 1972 to 1987. He presented a subjectwise and languagewise analysis of the dissertations submitted to the University. He was concluded that bibliographic organization of research work was not properly and adequately undertaken in the country. No systematic effort had been made to disseminate information on dissertations submitted to the universities and institutions.

It is concluded that the researches completed in the field of library history (1959) and classification (1968) are the examples of researches of that period. Research is always based on the changing need of the time. In this context, now a days documentation and information science is inspiring research trend in library and information science discipline.

Difficulties in securing posts immediately after leaving library schools and advantages or disadvantages of visiting speakers were not taken in the present study. Therefore no findings are obtained in this respect. Whatever findings are achieved by the researches, are original, reliable and valid in themselves.

Suggestions from Heads of the Departments

Suggestion from the heads of the departments of library and information science are mentioned in the following manner. These suggestions were invited from the heads of the departments of library and information science in the Indian universities for the improvement of library and information science education.

1. The syllabus of M.Lib.I.Sc. and B.Lib.I.Sc. course should be remodelled as per requirement.
2. The recommendations of U.G.C. panel on library and information science (1982) should be implemented.
3. Standards for admission to courses should be formulated.
4. The courses should be uniform in all the universities.
5. It should be integrated. Two years M.Lib.I.Sc. course ought to have been started.
6. Admissions should be make on merit basis.
7. All full time teachers should be appointed.
8. Teachers of library science must be professional having atleast 10 years' experience.
9. National Teachers' Training Institute should be established in this discipline.
10. Cataloguing from M.Lib.I.Sc. syllabus should be removed.
11. Practical at B.Lib.I.Sc. should be done according to one scheme of classification and one code of cataloguing.
12. Modern methods of teaching should be adopted such as—teaching through media, group discussion, Project method etc.

13. There should be an apprenticeship for atleast six months for the recognized libraries. Those students who have B.Lib.I.Sc. examination, degree should only be awarded when they have completed the apprenticeship programme and obtained certificate in this respect from the libraries.
14. Research in Library Information Science should be introduced at all schools.
15. There must be research fellowships in library and information science.
16. More contents of computer application should be introduced.
17. Inservice training should be given to the less qualified staff members.
18. Refresher courses should be orgainsed regularly to keep the librarians upto date.
19. Correspondence courses should be discountinued.
20. The programme of national exchange of teachers and appointment of visiting professors and fellows should be implemented in all the universities.
21. Semester system should be adopted for evaluation of the students.
22. U.G.C. should appoint a committee to examine/review the courses in the light of the recent developments in library and information science at least once in every two or three years.

Suggestions from the Researcher

1. The department of library and information science in universities should have Ph.D. (Library and Information Science) facility, M.Phil., M.Lib.I.Sc. and B.Lib.I.Sc. courses.
2. There should be an uniformity in minimum qualifications for admission to various courses.
3. The total number of seats in various courses in library

and information science should be fixed. The seats in M.Lib.I.Sc. and B.Lib.I.Sc. course should not exceed more than 12 and 31 to 40 candidates respectively.

4. Uniformity in reservation of seats should be maintained. The rules formulated by Central and State governments should be followed.
5. The criteria for selection of candidates should be on merit basis but the effective steps should be taken to see that only those with scholastic interest or aptitude enter the course.
6. The duration of M.Lib.I.Sc. and B.Lib.I.Sc. courses should not be more than one academic year. This uniformity should be maintained all over the country.
7. There should be uniformity in syllabus at M.Lib.I.Sc. and B.Lib.I.Sc. level in the states. Unit system in the syllabus should be adopted.
8. Teaching hours in the department of Library and Information Science should be day hours. The students do not get sufficient time to use the library and to solve their problems in morning and evening hours.
9. The average number of hours for M.Lib.I.Sc. and B.Lib.I.Sc. theory papers should be at least 24 per week for lecture. The U.G.C. review committee (1965) suggested 400 hours during a session comprising lectures, tutorials and class practicals to B.Lib.I.Sc. course. About one-half of these hours should be assigned to lectures and one-half of practicals. It is suggested 300–325 hours to M.Lib.I.Sc. course for lectures, tutorial and seminars.
10. The departments should arrange Seminars from time to time. The State governments should also provide financial assistance in addition to U.G.C. financial assistance.
11. The department should have all full time teachers. Alteast one professor, one reader and three lecturers

should be appointed in a department. U.G.C. guidelines should be followed in this respect.

12. The workload of teachers should be minimum as under:

    Professor—7 to 12 periods per week.

    Reader—13 to 18 periods per week.

    Lecturer—19 to 24 periods per week.

13. The qualification laid down by U.G.C. should be strictly followed for the appointment of teachers but the teachers of library and Information science are supposed to have the background of working experience of some years in libraries.

14. Modern methods of teaching should be adopted. Tele-lecture or tele-discussion methods may be followed for qualitative improvement in teaching. The new education policy 1985 has also suggested that the system has to be resurrected by fundamental changes in priorities, contents, methodologies of teaching and learning system of evaluation and management structures.

15. The teaching in Library and Information Science should be motivated through different medias and media effect on students must be recognized. Tapes and slides as one of the media for teaching in Library and Information Science are getting popularity in an effective manner, because it is easy to update the tape and slide materials while speed of presentation of materials is not complicated and the use of the material does not depend on the presence of a teacher. It can be used by the students also as and when they require.

16. Practical work in library should be done during the training period.

17. Correspondence courses should be discontinued and discouraged at all levels.

18. Refresher courses should be organized for teachers from time to time.

19. The annual examination question papers must be moderated by external and internal examiners.
20. The areas of research neglected should be taken for research on priority basis. More research facilities should be made available.
21. The regional languages should be encouraged as medium of instruction. Hindi is badly neglected as medium of instructions. It should be encouraged. The reading material in Hindi should be produced and brought to the notice of the students. If standard books in the subjects are available, teachers should not have any difficulty in Hindi as medium of instruction.
22. The department must have separate building with sufficient accommodation.
23. The department must have a library for the use of teachers and students. The heads of the department should be authorized to purchase books and periodicals. The departmental library should have sufficient budget for library. The U.G.C. review Committee had suggested a lump sum provision of Rs. 50,000=00 for basic books and a running provision of Rs. 8,000=00 per annum as the minimum requirement for department of library science.
24. The Central Library of the University should have sufficient collection of books and periodicals on library and information science.
25. The department of library and information science should be kept under the faculty of arts.
26. The programme of national exchange of teachers should be motivated and implemented.
27. The recommendations of U.G.C. panel on library and information science (1982) should be implemented.
28. The norms formulated for library and information science education should be implemented in the universities of Madhya Pradesh.

Suggestions for Further Research

There is a speedy development of library and information science education in India but its progress in research is somehow slow and its many aspects have been left for research. Three independent comprehensive studies should be taken to supplement or modify the conclusions of the present study.

1. A Comparative Study of Library and Information Science Education in India and United Kingdom.
2. Library and Information Science Education and Educational Technology—A study.
3. A Study of Librarian's Attitudes Towards Library and Information Science Education.
4. A Study of Job Satisfaction of College/Universities Librarians in India.
5. A Study of Budget Allocations for University Librarians in India.

APPENDICES

QUESTIONNAIRE

"A STUDY OF LIBRARY AND INFORMATION SCIENCE EDUCATION IN INDIAN UNIVERSITIES WITH A VIEW TO FORMULATE NORMS IN MADHYA PRADESH".

(Questionnaire to be filled by the Heads of the Department of Library and Information Science).

Directed by	*Conducted By :*
Dr. H.S. Sengar University Librarian Dr. Hari Singh Gour Vishwavidyalaya Sagar (M.P.)	Mr. B.P. Shrivastava Research Scholar Deptt. of Library and Information Science. Dr. H.S. Gour University, Sagar (M.P.)

Note : Please tick mark / for the answer you accept.

1. General Information

1.1. Name of the University/Institute/College

....

1.2 Year of the establishment of the department

....

1.3 Your Name ....

1.4 Status

Professor

University Librarian

Reader

Lecturer

Other

1.5 Age

Under 30

31 - 39

40 - 49

Above 50

1.6 Sex

Male

Female

1.7 What are your academic qualifications?

B.A./BSc./B.Com

M.A./M.Sc./M.Com.

B.Lib.I.Sc./Dip.Lib.Sc.

M.Lib.I.Sc.

Ph.D. (Lib.Sc.)

Ph.D. (other than

Library Science

2. Levels of Courses

2.1 What are the levels of courses in your university?

Ph.D.

M.Lib.I.Sc.

B.Lib.I.Sc.

Cert.Lib.Sc.

Any other course

2.2 What are the minimum qualifications for admission prescribed for each courses?

Ph.D.

M.Lib.I.Sc.

B.Lib.I.Sc.

Cert.Lib.Sc.

Any other course

2.3 What are the total seats for each course?

Ph.D.

M.Lib.I.Sc.

B.Lib.I.Sc.

Cert.Lib.Sc.

Any other course

2.4 Is there any reservation of seats for departmental candidates, scheduled caste, scheduled tribes, local and other university Candidates?

Yes No

2.5 If. yes, please show the percentage of seats reserved for these categories.

Deptt. candidates %

Scheduled Caste %

Scheduled Tribes %

Local %

Other Universities of the State %

Other Universities out of State %

Any other category %

2.6 What is procedure of selection of candidates for each course?

(a) On merit

(b) Merit-cum-Interview

(c) Written test-cum-Interview

(d) Only written test

2.7 Is there any procedure of selection applied to departmental candidates also?

Yes No

2.8 If no, what is the procedure of selection for departmental candidates?

(a) Deputed by the libraries

(b) On merit among departmental candidates

(c) Separate written test/interview.

(d) Any other procedure

2.9 What is the duration of period for each course?

M.Lib.I.Sc. month

B.Lib.I.Sc. month

Cert.Lib.Sc. month

Any other course month

2.9.1. Does your university run any Library science course through correspondence?

Yes No

2.9.2 If yes, what are levels of the courses with the duration?

M.Lib.I.Sc.	month
B.Lib.I.Sc.	month
Dip.Lib.I.Sc.	month
Cert.Lib.I.Sc.	month

3. Contents of Courses:

3.1 Please give below a complete list of compulsory and optional papers for each course

M.Lib.I.Sc.

1.	2.
3.	4.
5.	6.
7.	8.
9.	

B.Lib.I.Sc.

1.	2.
3.	4.
5.	6.
7.	8.

Cert.Lib.Sc.

1.	2.
3.	4.
5.	6.

3.2 Is there any uniformity of syllabus in your state?

M.Lib.I.Sc.	Yes	No
B.Lib.I.Sc.	Yes	No
Cert.Lib.Sc.	Yes	No

3.3 Is there unit system in the syllabus?

Yes No

3.4 Do you think the content of the syllabus in each course is insufficient or does it require any improvement? Kindly suggest measure for improvement in the content of the syllabus in each course.

....

....

....

3.5 Do you feel the need for organising some refresher courses for the practicing librarians. If so, kindly name the agency which should organise this course.

....

....

4. Examination:

4.1 What is the method of examination followed for each course?

M.Lib.I.Sc.	Annual examination Semester system.
B.Lib.I.Sc.	Annual examination Semester system.
Dip.Lib.Sc.	Annual examination Semester system.
Cert.Lib.Sc.	Annual examination Semester system.

4.2 Please give the maximum marks allotted for the examination for each course and the minimum prescribed for a first division, second division and a pass.

Course	*Max. Marks*	*Minimum for Ist Divn.*	*Minimum for IInd Divn.*	*Minimum for Pass*
M.Lib.I.Sc.				
B.Lib.I.Sc.				
Cert.Lib.Sc.				

4.3 Are the annual question paper moderated?

Yes No

4.4 If yes, by whom the question papers are moderated?

By external and the internal

By external only

By internal only

5. Research Facilities:

5.1 Do you have research familility for Ph.D. in library and Information Science?

Yes No

5.2 If so, what are the reasons for not having this facility?

(a) No post-graduation in library science

(b) No qualified guide

(c) No satisfactory library

(d) Other reason

5.3 If the research facilities are available, please give the number of Ph.D. degrees awarded and the research in progress.

Ph.D. awarded Research in progress

5.4 Please give the number of researches completed and research in progress.

(a) Library classification

(b) Library cataloguing

(c) Library organisation

(d) Library administration

(e) Reference service

(f) Documentation and Information Science

(g) Academic library

(h) Other

6. Teaching hours and Teaching Methods:

6.1 What are the teaching hours of the department?

Morning

Day

Evening

6.2 Please give the average number of hours per week for each course.

M.Lib.I.Sc.

B.Lib.I.Sc.,

Cert.Lib.Sc.

Any other

6.3 What are the methods of teaching adopted by the teachers? (Please give order or preference):

(a) Lecture

(b) Seminar

(*c*) Tutorial

(*d*) Apprenticeship

(*e*) Practical work

(*f*) Any other

6.4 What is the medium of instruction?

English

Hindi

Other

6.5 If the medium of instruction is Hindi, do you feel any difficulty in teaching?

Yes No

6.6 If yes, what difficulties do you feel? (give order of preference)

(*a*) Standard books in the subject are not available

(*b*) Technical words in Hindi are difficult

(*c*) Teachers are not well acquainted with the Hindi language

(*d*) Other

6.7 Did the department arrange seminars?

Yes No

6.8 If yes, how many seminars have been arranged so far?

Seminars.

7. Teaching Staff:

7.1 Do you have all full time teachers?

Yes No

7.2 If yes, please give the strength of the full time teachers?

Professor

Reader

Lecturer

Demonstrator

7.3 Please give academic qualifications of teachers?

(1)

(2)

(3)

(4)

(5)

(6)

(7)

(8)

(9)

(10)

7.4 What is the number of teachers guiding research work of students at Ph.D. level?

Teachers

7.5 Is there any research fellowship provided in library science? If so, give number.

Yes No Fellowship

7.6 If the department does not have full time teachers, please give the number of part-time teachers?

Teachers

7.7 Are they paid honourable for teaching?

7.8 If yes, please show the amount paid to them.

1. Rs. per month

2. % of their basic pay

3. Rs. per lecture

7.9 What is the workload of each teacher?

Professor periods per week

Reader periods per week

Lecturer periods per week

Part time Lecturer periods per week

Demonstrator periods per week

8. Physical Facilities :

8.1 Do you have separate building for the department or located within the library or located within some other department?

Separate building

Located within the library

Located within some other department

8.2 What is the accommodation in the department?

Lecture Rooms:

1 - 2 :

3 - 4 :

5 - 6 :

Room for practical work:

1

2

3

Room for seminar:

1

2

3

Room for students

1

2

Room for office work

1

2

Room for the Head of the Department

Room for staff

1

2

3

4

5

Other rooms

1

2

3

8.3 Are you satisfied with the space for the department?

Yes No

8.4 If the department is located within the library/some other department, do you feel any difficulty in your administration?

Yes No

8.5 If yes, what type of difficulties do you feel?

1

2

3

8.6 Does the department have all necessary teaching aids?

Most satisfactory

Satisfactory

Not satisfactory

9. Library Facilities:

9.1 Do you have departmental library?

Yes No

9.2 Who is incharge of departmental library?

Head of the department

Any other teacher

Full time trained person

A clerk

9.3 What is the procedure for the acquisition of books and periodicals for the departmental library?

(a) Centralized purchasing by the central library

(b) Head of the department authorised to purchase the books

(c) Loaned for the central library

(d) Other

9.4 What is annual average budget of the departmental library?

Rs. per annum

9.5 Are the books issued to the students and the staff from the departmental library?

Yes No

9.6 If yes, what is number of books issued to the students and the staff with the duration of period.

	No. of books	*Duration*
Undergraduate students		
Postgraduate students		

9.7 Is the collection of books in the departmental library sufficient to meet the requirements of the students and staff?

Most sufficient

Sufficient

Not sufficient

9.8 Is the collection of books and periodicals in the subject in central library sufficient?

Most sufficient

Sufficient

Not sufficient

10. Fees and Scholarships:

10.1 What are annual tuition fees for each course?

Ph.D.	Rs.
M.Lib.I.Sc.	Rs.
B.Lib.I.Sc.	Rs.
Cert.Lib.Sc.	Rs.
Any other	Rs.

11. Attendance:

11.1 What is the minimum percentage of attendance to appear in the annual examination?

Above 45%

Above 60%

Above 75%

Other

12. Faculty:

12.1 Under what faculty does your department comes?

Science	Arts
Humanities	Education
Technical Education	Social Sciences
Other	

SUGGESTIONS

Please give your personal suggestions for the improvement of Library and Information Science Education:

1.
2.
3.
4.
5.
6.
7.
8.
9.
10.

Signature

Name
Designation
University

BIBLIOGRAPHY

Agrawal, D.S., "Recommendations of review committee on library science: An evaluation". Her.Lib.Sci. 6, 1967: 167-74.

Agrawal, Y.P., Sampling methods for social investigation. Ambala, Bharat Vidya Vihar, 1976, p. 10.

Ahmad, Nasruddin. "Problems and perspects of library education in Bangladesh". Her.Lib.Sci. 30 (1-2), Jan.-April, 1991: 46-50.

Bar, Keith, ed. Essays on information and libraries: A festschrift for Donald Urquhart. London, Clive Bingley, 1975.

Bashiruddin, S., "Education for librarianship in India". Indian Libr. 17, Dec. 1972: 164-70.

Bhatia, S.R., "Libraries for library schools". In: Agrawal, S.N., Khan, R.R. and Satyanarayan, ed. Perspectives in library and information science, Vol. 2, Lucknow, Print House, 1982, pp. 85-88.

Bhargava, G.D., Librarianship in India and abroad: Restrospect and prospect. New Delhi, Metropolitan, 1977, p. 102.

Bobinski, George., "A survey of library schools", Jour. Edn. for Librarianship. 10(1) Summer 1969, pp. 39-43.

Bonn, George S., ed. Library education and training in developing countries. Honolulu, East West Press, 1966.

Borko, Harold, ed. Targets for research in library education. Chicago, American Library Association, 1973.

Bramley, Gerald, A history of library education. London, Clive Bingley, 1969.

Bramley, Gerald. World trends in library education, London, Clive Bingley, 1975.

Carnovsky, Leon, "Publishing the results of research in librarianship". Lib. Trends. 13(1) July, 1964: 126-40.

Chapman, Allan. Survey of methods of education and training for reference work. Abridged Report (Revised Version), 1970.

Chopra, H.R., "National policy on library and information science education". Her.Lib.Sci. 24(1-2) Jan-April, 1985: 70-74.

Chopra, H.R., "Study of librarianship as a profession in India". In: Gupta, Pawan K., ed. Library and Information science: a current trends in India, Jaipur, RBSA Publishers, 1986, pp. 85-96.

Danton, J.P., Education for librarianship. Paris, Unesco, 1949, pp. 5-6.

Danton, J.P., "Doctoral studies in librarianship in the United States". Coll.Res.Libs. 20(6)/Nov. 1959, 435-53.

Dean, John, "Training and management for library personnel: professional education in Nigeria". Nigerian Libraries 2(2). Sept. 1966: 70.

Dennis, Laurent G., "A study of the need for Ph.Ds in library science in large Canadian libraries". Canadian Library Journal 29(1) Jan. 1972: 19-27.

Department of Education and Science, Library Advisory Councils of England and Wales, Report on the supply and training of lbrarians (Joseph report). London, H.M. S.O. 1968.

Deshpande, A.L., "Improving teaching in higher education", University News., 29(49) Dec. 1991: 1 & 24.

Devarajan, G., "Recent trends at the post-graduate level researches in library and information science in India", Luck, Libn. 20(1) 1988: 26-32.

Eaton, A.J., "Research in librarianship in U.S.A." Libri. 21, 1971: 350-60.

Eaton, Thelma, "Bibliographical research" Lib. Trends 13(1) July 1964: 42-53.

Encyclopedia of Librarianship. Landu, Thomas. ed. 3rd ed. Calcutta, Rupa, 1967, p. 159.

Encyclopedia of Library and Information Science. Kent, Allen. and Paily Jay E., ed. New York, Marcal Dekker, 1974, Vol. 11, 99. pp. 312-49.

Foskett, A.C., A new approach to teaching classification and Cataloguing. Jou.Edn.Libr. 10(4) Spring, 1970: 276-282.

Ghanchi, D.A., "New directions of teaching at higher level" in Ruhela, S.P. and Singh, R.P., ed. Trends in modern Indian education. New Delhi, Uppal, 1990: pp. 153-161.

Ghose, S.B., Library science in India; A study of manpower and educational programme. New Delhi, Insdoc, 1972. (Unpublished project report.)

Good, William J., Methods in social research, New York, McGraw Hills, 1952.

Goyal, Saty Paul, ed. Indian Librarianship. Delhi, Scientific Book store, 1972.

Goyal, Saty Paul, "An experiment in M.Lib.I.Sc. teaching". Her. Lib.Sci. 20(1-2) Jan.-Apr. 1981: 49-54.

Grotzinger, Laurel, "The status of 'practicum' in graduate library schools. Jour. Edn. Libn. 11(4) Spring, 1971: 338-39.

Gujrati, Balwant Singh, ed. Readings in library science. Ludhiana, Lyall Book Depot. 1968, pp. 16-33.

Gupta, P.K., "Educational needs of professional library workers and L & I.S. education in India". In Gupta, P.K. ed. Library and Information Science: Current Trends in India. Jaipur, RBSA Publishers, 1986, pp. 52-77.

Harlow, Neal Rotan, "Doctoral study: Key to what", Coll.Res.Libs. 29(6) Nov. 1968: 485.

ILA-IASLIC-GILA-IATLIS Library Education Centenary Seminar, Nagpur, Oct. 1987—Report.

India, Advisory Committee for Libraries. (1958), Report 2nd ed. Delhi, Manager of Publications, 1960, pp. 86-102.

India, Education Commission, 1964-66, Report, Delhi, Manager of Publications, 1966 (Chairman: D.S. Kothari).

India, Ministry of Human Resource Development, Committee on National Policy on Library and Information System (1985). National policy on library and information system: a presentation. New Delhi, 1986, 30 p. (Mimeographed).

India, Ministry of Education, Challenges of education: a policy perspective. Delhi, Manager of publications, 1985, pp. 71-72.

Issac, K.A., "Need for new directions in teaching of library science" In: Seminar, Librarianship and information science in Zool, Madras, British Council Library, 1975, pp. 91-105.

Jaohda, Gerald, "Education for information science". Annual Rev. In.Sc. Techn. 8, 1973, pp. 321-44.

Kapoor, Malti M., "Education for librarianship in Indian Universities with special reference to pattern of entrants-survey report". Ann.Lib.Sci. Documn. 15(2) June 1968: 76-102.

Kapoor, R.P. and Ravinder Kaur, "Current trends in Library Science Education in India". LIBR 17-18, 1978-79; 79-80; 71-78.

Kapoor, S.K. and Banerjee, S.N, "Education for library and information science: need for a rational approach." IASLIC Bull. 31(2) 1986: 63-71.

Kaula, P.N., Library education in India. In Kaula, P.N., ed. Library movement in India. Delhi, Delhi Library Association, 1958, pp. 42-49.

Kaula, P.N., "Library Schools in India". Her.Lib.Sci. 5, 1966 : 308-11.

Kaula, P.N., "Evaluation of education for librarianship in India", UNESCO Bull, 21, 1967: 182-89.

Kaula, P.N., "Hundred years of library and information science education : evaluation and trend". Her.Lib.Sci. 27(3-4) July-Oct. 1988: 170-77.

Kister, Kenneth F., "Educating librarians in intellectual freedom. Lib.Trends 19(1) July 1970: 159-68.

Kolhatkar, M.R. 'Some issues relating to eighth five year-plan educational sector". Journal of Education and Social change 4(2) July-Sept. 1990, p. 6.

Krishnamurthy, C.S., "Education for librarianship". Lib.Hen. 5N (3-4) Oct.-Jan. 1962-63: 131-39.

Kumar, P.S.G., Comp. Research in library and information science, indexed by A. Tejomurthy and H.R. Chopra. New Delhi. Concept Publishing, 1987.

Kumar, P.S.G., "Hundred years of library education". Her.Lib.Sci. 26(1-2), Jan.-April, 1988: 81-88.

Lamkin, Burton E., "Towards a federal strategy in library training". Amer.Lib. 2(5) May 1971: 497.

Library and Information Service Council, London. Professional education and training for library and information work: a review. London, LISC, 1986.

Mangla, P.B., "Levels of training in library and information science: admission requirements and duration". Lib.Sci. with Slant to DOC. 15, 1978: 125-31.

Mangla, P.B., Library and Information Science Education in India : Papers and Recommendations, Delhi, Macmillan, 1981, XXIII, pp. 345.

Mangla, P.B., Research in Library and Information Science in U.S.A., U.K. and India: An Overview. In: Agrawal, S.N., Khan. R.R., and Satyanarayan, N.R., ed. Perspectives in Library and Information Science, Vol. 2, Lucknow, Print Hose, 1982, pp. 44-61.

Mangla, P.B., "Library Education in India, Pakistan and Bangladesh". Advances in Librarianship, 10, 1986: 191-240.

Mangla, P.B., "Research in library and information science and the contribution of Ranganathan". Education for Information, 2, 1984: 267-82.

Mangla, P.B., "Workshop on the Methods of Teaching and Evaluation in Library Science: A Report". IASLIC Bull, 18, 1973: 115-38.

Mangla, P.B., "Library and Information Science Education in India: Rends and Issues". University News. 28(24) June 1990: 7-15.

Macro, Guy, "Doctoral Programmes in American Library Schools". Jour. Edn. Librarianship, 8(1) Summer, 1967: 6-13.

Meetings of the Supervisors of Library and Documentation Schools in Asian Region (Banglore) (1976). Library and information manpower development in the Asian region: report, Banglore, DRTC, 1976.

Mittal, R.L. "Teaching of Library Science in India". Libri. 17(4), 1967: 252-69.

Mitra, N.L., "Reservation in admission to higher academic courses: a bundle of judicial confusion". University News, 29(49), Dec. 1991: 4-7.

Mohanty, Jagannath, "Higher education: methods and media". University News. 28(24) June 1990: 1-2, 6.

Neelameghan, A., "India, education for librarians and documentalists in". In Encylopedia of Library and Information Science, ed. by Allen Kent and Harold Lancour. New York, Marcel Dekker, Vol. 11, 1974, pp. 312-349.

Neelameghan, A. "Guidelines for formulating policy on education, training and development of library and information personnel. Paris, Unesco, 1978.

Odhams Dictionary of English Language. Smith, A.H. and O'Louglin, J.L.N., ed. Watford, Odhams, n.d.

Palmer, B.I., Development of education for librarianship in Britain. In: Goyal Sat Paul. Indian librarianship : essays in honour of S.R. Bhatia. Delhi, Scientific Book Store, 1972, pp. 119-30.

Pancholi, A.L., Foundations of research methodology. Jaipur, Publications Scheme, 1988.

Prashar, R.G., ed. University libraries in India 1980s and beyond: essays in honour of T.P. Saxena. New Delhi, Medallian Press, 1991.

Prasher, R.G., Managing University Libraries, New Delhi, Today & Tomorrow's Printers and Publishers, 1991, pp. 224-27.

Prasher, R.G., Information and its communication. New Delhi, Medallion Press, 1991, pp. 211-17.

Ram Tirth and Kamleshwar Nath, "Library science education in Indian Universities". Her.Lib.Sci.6, 1967: 158-66.

Ranganathan, S.R., "Training for librarianship". Ann.Lib.Sci. 5, 1950: 55.

Ranganathan, S.R., "Perits of library education". Libra, 1966-67: 1.

Ranganathan, S.R., "Future of library service and library science in India". Her.Lib.Sci. 7, 1968: 1-8.

Rao, Dittakavi Nagasankara, "Comparative study of library science education in the United States and India". Her.Lib.Sci. 20(1-2) Jan.-Apr. 1981: 43-49.

Rao, I.K., Ravichandra, Quantitative methods for library and information science, New Delhi, Willey Eastern, 1983.

Rao, Ram Krishna, K., "Preparation of librarians in India. Lib.Quarterly 33, July 1963: 242-52.

Robbins, Marry Esther, "Inspection of library training schools, 1914". In Seavey, Charles. A., ed. Occasional papers, No. 186, Urbana: University of Illinois, Graduate School of Library Information Science, 1989, p. 87.

Sabor, Josepha, Methods of teaching librarianship. Paris, UNESCO, 1969.

Saunders, W.L., "Professional education: Some challenges for the next decade". In: Bar, Keith and Line, Maurice, ed. Essays on

Information and Libraries: A Festschrift for Donal Urquhart London, Clive Bingley, 1975, pp. 151-52.

Saunders, W.L., "Education for librarianship" In Whatley, H.A., ed. British Librarianship and information science 1966-1970. London, Library Association, 1972, pp. 268-91.

Waunders, W.L., "The nature of information science". The Information Scientist 8(2) June, 1974: 57-70.

Seminar on Teaching of Library Science (Delhi) (1966). Papers and recommendations: University of Delhi, Department of library science, 1966 (Mimeographed).

Seager, Daniel A., "To maintain quality". Jour. Edn. Libn. 4(1) Summer, 1963: 27-39.

Seetharama, S., "Library and information science research in India: analytical study based on the input to ISORTD. Lib.Sci. Documn. 13, Sept.-Dec. 1976: 126.

Sharma, B.A.V., Research methods in social sciences. New Delhi, Sterling, 1983, pp. 4-5, 147.

Shah, S.Y. ed., New Technologies in higher education, New Delhi, Association of Indian Universities, 1986.

Shera, J.H., "Drawin Bacon and research in librarianship". Lib. Trends 13(1) July 1964: 141-49.

Shera, J.H., Foundations of education for librarianship. New York, Becker and Hayer, 1972.

Shukla, R.K., "Library science teaching for semiprofessionals: Some observations in medium of instruction" Luck. Libn. 19(1) 1987: 11-15.

Singh, Ramjee, "Library schools in India: an Observation". LIBRA 1966-67: 35-42.

Singh, Jagtar, "Accreditation of LIS programmes in India" In : Prasher, R.G. ed. University libraries in India: 1980s and beyond—essays in honour of T.P. Saxena. New Delhi, Medallion Press, 1991, pp. 241-47.

Srivastava, S.N., University libraries in India, by S.N. Shrivastava and S.C. Verma, New Delhi, Sterling, 1980.

Srivastava, S.N., "Qualitative improvement in LIS education", In: Prasher, R.G., ed. University Libraries in India: 1980s and beyond essays in honour of T.P. Saxena. New Delhi, Medallion Press, 1991, pp. 248-55.

Srivastava, S.S., Survey research techniques. Allahabad, Chaitanaya Publishing House, 1971, pp. 1, 71.

Smith, Gerald R., "Inadequacies in research proposals" Lib. Trends 13(1) July 1964: 68-83.

Tejomurty, A., "Research in library and information science". In: Bhargava, G.D. and Tejomurty, A. ed. Dimensions in library and information science. Indore, Anamika Publications, 1986, pp. 99-112.

Tejomurty, A., Master of library and information science dissertations at Vikram University from 1972 to 1987. Her. Lib.Sci. 27 (N 3-4) July-Oct. 1988: 192-95.

Tony, Bernard J., "Indian library science training, 1911-65" Jour. edn. Libn. 8, 1967: 111-23.

Trautman, Ray, A history of school of library service, Columbia University, New York, Columbia University Press, 1954.

Umapathy, K. Setty, "Education for librarianship" In: Goyal, Sat Paul, ed. Indian librarianship: essays in honour of S.R. Bhatia, Delhi, Scienttific Book Store, 1972, pp. 1-12.

University Grants Commission (India), Review Committee (1965). Library Science in Indian Universities, New Delhi, U.G.C., 1965 86 p.

University Grants Commission (India), Panel on library and information science, recommendations. New Delhi, U.G.C., 1982 (Mimeographed).

University Grants Commission (India), Inter Agency Working Group, Development of an information and library network: Report. New Delhi, U.G.C., 1988, XXX, pp. 473.

UNESCO, World guide to library schools and training courses in documentation. London, Clive Bingley, 1972.

UNESCO, Report of a meeting of supervisors of library and documentation schools in the Asian Region, Banglore, India 9-12 Nov. 1976, Paris, UNESCO, 1977.

Venkatappaiah, V., ed. March of library science: papers in honour of P.N. Kaula, New Delhi, Vikas Publishing House, 1979.

Vidyarthi, L.P., Research methodology in social science in India. New Delhi, Today and Tomorrow's Printers, 1985.

Ward, P.L., ed. Introduction guide to research in library and information studies, ed. by P.L. Ward, Burnett and P. Whiteman, ed. London, Library Association, 1975.

White, Herbert S. and Mort, Sarah L., The accredited library education program as preparation for professional library work. Lib. Quarterly 60(3), July 1990: 187-215.

Williams, P. Havard, "Library and information education in Britain". In: Agrawal, S.N., Khan, R.R. and Satyanarayan, N.R., ed. Perspectives in library and information science. Vol. 2, Lucknow, Print House, 1982, p. 72-84.

Williams, P. Harvard, "LIS Curriculum : A Model" In:" Bhargava, G.D. and Tejomurty, A., ed. Dimensions in library and information science. Indore, Anamika Publications, 1986, pp. 1-34.

Williams, V. Akinyele, "Members forum: institute of librarianship is impractical", Nigerian Libraries 5(1) Apr. 1969: 26-28.

Yelland, M., Research in librarianship: British librarianship and information science 1966-70. London, Library Association, 1972, pp. 309-319.

INDEX

V

W